CONCILIUM

Theology in the Age of Renewal

CONCILIUM

Theology in the Age of Renewal

Volume 51: Dogma

Dogma and Pluralism

Edited by
Edward Schillebeeckx

Herder and Herder

1970
HERDER AND HERDER
232 Madison Avenue, New York 10016

Cum approbatione Ecclesiastica

Library of Congress Catalog Card Number: 74–98258

Printed in the United States

CONTENTS

Editorial

THE tensions within the Catholic Church in matters of doctrine and discipline have assumed critical proportions. Those who before were hardly interested in Church affairs, now often appear to be deeply involved in them. They hope that through being plunged into the great spiritual upheaval of our time, the Church may regain relevance. On the other hand, those who deplore the way in which renewal has been expressed often find the tension almost intolerable. Some of them see only erosion, disintegration and loss of identity, and, tired of it all, withdraw into a self-imposed isolation or, in their disappointment, turn away from the Church altogether.

This last reaction is understandable, but it misinterprets the true nature of these tensions. When all is said and done, the struggle for new structures and norms in our life and thought are proof of the vitality of the ecclesial community.

Community does not merely consist in a passive consent to what others are saying and doing, and have said and done in the past. True community implies the courage to bring profound differences of opinion into the open. It is able to bear these differences in the interests of the renewal of communal vitality, and of the new life which, according to Scripture, is the hallmark of the believer.

This issue of *Concilium* hopes to make some modest contribution to man's sense of direction in this painful but inevitable process. It therefore concentrates on some points that, at the moment, stand in the centre of doubt and controversy: orthodoxy, heresy and pluralism, and the oneness of the faith.

It begins with a highly personal statement. Morris West explains some of the causes of his unease: the growing self-awareness of modern man who finds authoritarianism increasingly intolerable; the lack of mutual support within the ecclesial community; and the erosion of the freedom that is essential to the personal practice of one's faith.

Myles Bourke shows in the next article that the most drastic means of ensuring the unity of the faith, excommunication, can still be applied in principle but is difficult to justify by an appeal to Scripture. The use of dialogue, as initiated by Vatican II, is far more appropriate.

One of the means by which the early Church tried to preserve and consolidate this oneness of the faith was the drafting of creeds and rules of faith. These originated in the instructions for baptism and the context of the eucharistic celebrations. The doctrinal divisions which arose in the early Church led to the formulation of brief summaries of the basic elements of Christian doctrine (Brekelmans).

The function of the *magisterium* also has to be re-examined. It is exercised by various kinds of authority in the Church and should be concerned also with the deeper causes of the existing tensions. The *magisterium* must therefore be prepared to practise this dialogue and to recognize the theologian's proper function (Gutwenger).

Because of the historicity of Christianity the matter of orthodoxy or heterodoxy cannot be decided merely by reference to an absolutely fixed rule of faith. Varied and simultaneous developments in the Christian reflection on faith can occur because they are conditioned by different sets of circumstances. These developments, however, demand some sort of balance so that they all correspond to the various aspects of the mystery which is the ultimate object of the Christian faith. When this balance is broken, the Christian community will be forced to make a choice (Jossua).

We ought to realize, however, that such notions as revelation or tradition do not have to be understood as the Greek distinction between action and contemplation has led them to be understood. As Martin Buber and Blondel had pointed out already, encounter, commitment and orthopraxis are important categories which were pushed into the background by a purely intellectual approach to the faith (Dupuy).

A formulation of the faith ought to reflect both the personal experience of the faith and the possibility of communicating with the other *as other* within the community. This is the only way of avoiding personal unauthenticity and the flight into spiritual isolation (de Certeau).

The present tensions within the Church are also caused by the fact that insufficient attention is paid to the *implicit* points of agreement in the existing pluralistic situation. God's Word operates in more fields than we are aware of. This means that the notion of orthodoxy must be understood in a positive and dynamic sense, so that it fits in with what Bergson called the *société ouverte* (Pinto de Oliveira).

The last two contributions show that these tensions are not limited to the Catholic Church. The Churches of the Reformation are also involved. In Germany, this disquiet centres round the implications of Bultmann's existential theology, but these doubts and worries rarely penetrate to the real core of Bultmann's meaning. The protest coming from opposite sides seem to lead to spiritual isolation (Dietzfelbinger).

In England the tensions within Anglicanism were pushed to the fore by the writings of Dr John Robinson. The situation in the United States is more complicated. A period of neo-orthodoxy was succeeded during the last decade by a dramatic upheaval, of which the controversies round the death-of-God theology were the most striking feature (Allchin).

PART I
ARTICLES

Morris L. West

Causes of Disquiet in the Church

THE Church is, just now, a discontented assembly. It is discontented because it is alive—and, like every living organism, is subject to the painful dynamic of birth, growth, decay and regeneration.

I am a member of the assembly. I am content in the faith—my act of acknowledgment of mystery and of Christ as the solution and summation of the mystery. I am very unhappy with the state of affairs in the assembly. I see great dangers in it—not for myself, because I am old enough to have come to terms with imperfection—but for my children and for the world which they have inherited.

Why am I unhappy? Why are so many others unhappy? Why do so many rebel, defect or lapse into the indifference of total frustration? Here, I believe, are some of the reasons.

1. *Increasing Self-Awareness*

People are more aware of their "self-hood" than they ever were before. They know more about their bodily functions, more about the intricacies of their psyche than their forefathers. As a consequence, they are more aware of the mystery of the self. The more they are aware of mystery, the less they are prepared to accept draconic solutions to the human dilemma or pat answers to the questions which plague them every hour.

A papal encyclical, written in the formal and sterile style of the courts, makes no impression on the poignantly involved self. A half-hour sermon on Sunday, didactic or hortatory, leaves the self still solitary. Ten minutes in the confessional for a ritual recital of faults, a ritual counselling, a ritual absolution, is small solace for a self haunted by the horrors of our time—tyranny and mass murder, and hunger, and the conspiracies of violence.

I am a self. I have begotten other selves. How do we survive, sane and human, in a madness of animals?

2. *Increasing Isolation of the Self*

We selves are becoming more and more isolated in this century of the conglomerates. We have long since been detribalized. Now, in the great cities, we are being defamilialized—an ugly and artificial word for an ugly and unnatural situation. We live apart in boxes called apartments. We bore peep-holes in the door to spy out hostile intruders. The capitalist economy forces us to be competitive. The socialized economy makes us rivals in a bureaucracy. The self is forced to become a function in the collective. The collective fears the self. The self, in fear or hatred of the collective, either withdraws into a foetal dark, or explodes outward in a revolutionary crisis.

3. *Increasing Risks for the Self*

Either way, the risks are enormous. The self-in-fugue has no point of arrival except a dark corner of a dark room, where it huddles, blind, deaf and dumb, paralysed with fear of nameless horrors. The self-in-revolt fragments itself in anger, lust and violence until all the king's horses and all the king's men—and all the therapists in the world—cannot put it together again.

The risks to the self grow greater every day as new energies are released by scientific discovery, and mass-communication and geo-political changes. The reaction against the risks grows stronger, too. Violence creates conspiracy. Conspiracy begets fear and fragmentation. And the self-at-risk, for want of other fraternity, throws itself into the conflict. It is the terror of our times. We try to survive by destruction.

4. *The Lack of Familial Affirmation in the Church*

It is precisely in this crisis that the great defect of today's Church is made visible: the lack of a simple, familial affirmation.

Like it or not, admit it or not, we are brothers and sisters in a human family. Some of us have been given a gift—the gift of being able to accept Jesus of Nazareth as the Son of God and the deliverer of a saving message for our selves and all other human selves.

This gift makes us a family within a family. It imposes new familial obligations on us, but it does not absolve us from those we already have. We are committed to a belief in Christ, a hope in his redemptive mediation, and a love, in, through and with him, for the human family. All else is method and methodology —a conflict of authorities, a dialectic of theologians, a clash of canonists. We are impoverished and not enriched by it.

We selves are the Church—we human selves in union with the human-divine self of Christ. We are the assembly, and the assembly exists for us, not we for it. . . . "Who for us men and for our saving came down from heaven."

Let me make the argument very personal. I have created a family, built a household about it. I am its head, but not its master. We, the separate selves, are the primal assembly. We have a mutual need of care, respect and love. We regulate ourselves; but the regulation is to the end of love and nurture. We have, in the broadest sense, a common faith, a common moral code. But the faith is shared in love; and the meaning of its tenets is debated with love and a desire for enlarged knowing. If we breach the moral code, our concern is to repair the breach and hold the love intact. Without the breach, the love might never be tested, perhaps never known.

So, we are jealous of the code, but tolerant of the breach. We know that we or our children can so tangle our lives that we may have to live for years with an anomalous situation—a bad marriage, a liaison, an illegitimate child. We do not drive out the offenders. We do not pass draconic judgments, impose lifelong sanctions. The self—the thing God made—has to be preserved and helped to grow to the fullest maturity—salvation—of which it is capable.

Today's Church functions more like a corporation than a family. The hierarchic form of the family is there, but the family life takes place elsewhere. I know my bishop as a photograph in a newspaper, the signatory of an occasional pastoral letter. He makes decisions in which I have no part. He lives in a "palace" by a "cathedral". He is no longer a pastor, a shepherd, but a president, treating with me through a priesthood, as a bureaucrat treats with me through an army of clerks. I do not blame him. The organization has dehumanized him by separating him from his flock. There are too many of us, too few of him. He was appointed over us. We did not "choose him to ourselves" for his talent, his care and his capacity for spiritual service. He is out of touch with us and we with him. And this is the next major cause of discontent.

5. *Breakdown of Communications within the Church Family*

The Roman Catholic assembly no longer functions as a Christian family, because communication within it has been broken down. We, the faithful, are legislated for, written to, talked at, talked about, mourned over, prayed over, censured as subjects or objects of scandal, as though we were the proles in some vast crypto-Christian socialist State. We have no voice in the assembly of selves. *De facto*, our true relationship is denied: self-to-God, in union with the other selves who have the same relationship.

The Church, centred in Rome, has succumbed to typically Roman illusions: that order can be imposed by legislation, that faith can be kept pure by multiplying definitions, that unity is best preserved by centralization, that authority must be as jealously guarded, as sedulously inflated, as the *numen* of the ancient emperors.

Family experience, community experience, point to quite opposite conclusions. When laws are multiplied, the law falls into disrepute. Language is an imperfect instrument of communication and we are forced constantly to supplement its imperfections by subsidiary codes. The specialized language of theologians and philosophers embalms an idea like a bee in amber; but the bee is dead. We assent to a living Christ and a living revelation by an act of belief unlimited by human verbalisms. The verbalisms are unstable and, in time, become irrelevant without constant gloss and interpretations. Unity—"the unity of the Spirit in the bond of faith"—is not necessarily preserved by a central organization of guardians.

My act of faith is a free assent to Christ and to his revelation. I cannot be forced to make it. I cannot be forced to withdraw it, by a central authority. The act itself joins me to the community of believers, and establishes the continuing communion between us. Whatever authority is established within the assembly is established by and through the assembly, which is itself in union with Christ.

The pope is elected—chosen—by the assembly. The voice of the assembly is the only voice of Christ left to us to make this act of election. The ritual of papal election affirms this fact. *"Acceptasne electionem?"*—"Do you accept the choice *we* have made?"

It has been too long forgotten that the pastor is chosen by the faithful, for the service of the faithful who reside "in the unity of the faith". The unity of the faith is already established. It does not and cannot depend upon the authority of the pastor. The concept of Christian authority as something imposed upon the faithful is essentially unchristian. Christ's presentation of himself was in the form of an invitation—"Come, follow me." The sum of his teaching was love, communion, communication—the free gift of the self to the Other and the others.

It seems to me, therefore, that the true function of authority within the Church is to recall the faithful constantly to the union of love which they themselves establish by their common assent to Christ and his teaching. In the earliest Church, the *kerygma* came first and the *didachè* grew out of it. Without the *kerygma*, the *didachè* reduces itself to a system of ethics as unstable as the customs of men in their changing habits and habitats.

6. *A Sense of the Inadequacy of Logic and Legalism*

What is under challenge today in the Church is not the "teaching of the Kingdom of God", but some of the interpretations of that teaching, the logic upon which the interpretation is based, and the laws by which it is enforced. To quote a simple example. All the marriage legislation of the Church is dominated by a legal norm laid down by Innocent III—*favor matrimonii*. If the validity of the bond is in doubt, the bond and not the person or persons must be favoured. Why? Man, and not an institution is the object of salvation. Is his salvation helped or hindered by a norm laid down to preserve public order? The question is urgent for many and reasonable for all. Why should it not be asked, debated, hotly contested?

A reigning pope decides that he will close or forbid discussion upon certain vital issues, reserve to himself the right of decision upon them. The matters touch us, the faithful, most intimately. They touch us in our lives and after-lives. We believe in the working of the Spirit, but we do not believe in illuminism and we are sceptical about private revelations. We ask, with deep concern, who is counselling the pontiff upon these matters of life, death and salvation, who, if anybody, represents to him our knowledge and experience of all the tangled issues involved, who monitors for us the logic and the legalities of his decision? We remember wryly that the marriage courts have a personage who is called *Defensor Vinculi*, but that there is no *Defensor Personae*. We need a voice for the People of God so that they may be heard in the councils of the Servant of the Servants of God. The act of faith is not made once for all. It is renewed daily and it must be renewed, as it was made, freely, with the full exercise of reason and with the deepest possible knowledge.

The apostolic authority is conferred by election. But the nature and the limits of apostolic authority are still a subject of legitimate discussion. Still more must the exercise of the authority be subject to discussion and scrutiny—and sometimes to challenge. Even St Paul withstood the Prince of the Apostles to his face. We are not driven to salvation like sheep. We accept it as a gift of eternal love by a knowing act. Therefore, the knowing is all-important to us. Therefore we are chary when the logic of theologians is based on presumptions, and when laws are based on concepts of the human person which are not yet beyond question.

A critic is not a traitor, though he may be an uncomfortable member of the Mystical Body. A questioner is not a rebel. His questions are the symptom of his concern for the truth. Religion is that which binds a man, because he chooses to be bound. It is not a serfdom. It is the liberty of the sons of God.

7. *A Fundamental Desire for Christian Liberty*

Liberty is a state to be attained and a burden to be borne. The assent of faith is a liberating act because it establishes a direction of growth for the human person, a conformity between himself and his fellows, which is based on his conformity with the living Christ. However, the limits of liberty, like the limits of authority, are still not clearly defined; and a desire for order and uniformity in the Christian assembly is not sufficient reason either for defining them too rigidly or for holding to certain too rigid definitions which have already been made.

Once again, we are face to face with a specifically Roman concept—that the object of all law is public order and not the dispensation of justice to individuals. Canon law is Roman to its foundations. It is loaded in favour of institutions and against individuals. It is, we are told, in process of reform, but the concepts upon which it is based need as radical a review as the *Codex* itself.

But how do we, the subjects of the law, bring about this so necessary review? How do we join a vital debate with the ecclesiastical Commissioners who will frame the new canons? We have no direct communication with them, no hope of a dialogue. So, we publish opinions, we stir up discussions. Some of us breach what we believe are bad laws in the hope of persuading the legislators to frame better ones.

I do not believe that every protestor is a schismatic or a rebel or a source of scandal. Neither do I believe that every prudent conservator is a tyrannical reactionary. However, I do believe that certain primitive Christian principles must be shouted over and over from the roof-tops. The interpreters of the Word are servants of the Word. Every one of us, pope, bishop, priest, layman or laywoman, is a servant of his brothers and sisters in Christ. The law is made for man, not man for the law. The union of Christ with his people is a mystical marriage. It is not a bed of Procrustes, on which the agony of humankind is extended to an intolerable infinity.

We are with Christ. We are with Peter, to whom our Lord gave primacy among those he sent. But—God help us!—where do we stand and how do we cope with some of Peter's secretaries!

8. *Sterility in the Liturgical Life of the Church*

There is a blight of sterility upon the whole liturgical life of the Church. I use the word liturgical in its broadest sense to describe every public activity within the assembly—the ritual, the administration of sacraments, the Mass, the practice of priestly and religious life, missionary activity, hierarchic administration.

In every sector of Church life we are locked into forms which, by centuries of use, have assumed a pseudo-sacral character. Many of the forms are associated with wealth, clerical privilege, ecclesiastical theatre, triumphalism, monarchy, exclusivity and vestigial superstition. In so far as they are aids to piety or identification or associative loyalty, they have a value, but to defend them as if they were the last bastions of belief is dangerous and confusing.

It is all too easy to censure the excesses of innovating ritualists, who are more preoccupied with the theatre of religion than with its substance. It is too easy to praise them as noble revolutionaries stamping out the last traces of superstition in the two-thousand-year-old assembly. Rites and reverences are human devices, human symbols, to express and to aid the transcendental relationship between creature and creator. Like all things human, they must be treated with respect, but never allowed to become obstacles to the spiritual communion between men of goodwill.

Celibacy and virginity are physical states until individuals make a virtue of them. Marriage is a social contract—successful or unsuccessful—until faith and charity endow it with the transcendental character of a sacrament. A man is ordained to priesthood and commissioned to the ministry of the Word. If he is incompetent or unwilling for either, he must be released with dignity and charity. There can be as much scandal in the sanctions of the canons as in the personal failures of clerics and religious.

Conclusion

To sum up: ritual is an aid to and a method for the practice of the believers' life of charity. Authority is an instrument for the service of the assembly of believers; dogma is a codification—in human, and therefore imperfect terms—of the substance of faith; teaching and interpretation represent the Christian effort to apply Revelation to human life in its swiftly changing circumstances.

Man is the object of them all—man, capable of self-destruction, capable, too, of self-salvation by an act of love for himself, his fellows and for his Creator in whom they and he subsist.

The tensions in the assembly begin when institutions are set above men. They will subside when man assumes the place God gave him, son-ship and brotherhood in the family.

Myles M. Bourke

Should the Church impose Sanctions for Errors of Faith?

BECAUSE of the function of the Scriptures in the life of the Church, it is imperative that the Bible be consulted in attempting to answer the question posed in the title of this article. Obviously, such an investigation is a useless exercise in the opinion of those who regard the Scriptures as documents of a past age which have little to say to those who now follow the guidance of the Spirit. Such persons take a low view of the normative character of the Bible, speaking of it as a collection of "historically conditioned" books. But "historically conditioned" ought not to be used as a synonym for "outmoded". Paul's order that women should pray only with veiled heads is historically conditioned; so too are Amos's words on the oppression of the poor. Whether biblical statements are merely the reflection of a superseded *Zeitgeist*, or have enduring validity, is a matter which has to be settled on other grounds than that they bear the mark of their times.

The Bible does not attest with any frequency to the invoking of sanctions against those members of the community who interpret the faith in a manner which the community rejects. There is clear indication in both Old and New Testaments that exclusion from the community was used as a penalty, but in the majority of cases it was a penalty for moral offences, and in other respects, as well, was different from the excommunication with which the later Church punished those of her members who had erred in matters of faith. The *anathema* of the Councils bears only a slight resemblance, if any, to that of the Old Testament or even to that of Paul.

I. Exclusion from the Community in the Old Testament

The Septuagint uses *anathema* to translate the Hebrew *ḥerem*, a term applied to a person or thing set apart from profane circumstances or uses and consecrated to God. In a few instances the setting apart is a consecration as a sacred gift or sacrifice (cf. 2 Mac. 2. 13; 9. 16; Jud. 16. 19; this usage is also found in Lk. 21. 5). But usually it was a consecration to the divine wrath, and was expressed by destruction. Normally, this penalty affected non-Israelites and thus had nothing to do with exclusion from the community of Israel; the population and the property of the cities of Canaan were put under the *ḥerem* by the invading Israelites (cf. Num. 21. 3; Deut. 7. 25 f.; Jos. 6. 17).

Yet that was not always the case. Israelites who violated the *ḥerem* invoked on Jericho were themselves put under it (cf. Jos. 6. 18; 7. 12); in Deuteronomy 13. 15, it is invoked against Hebrews guilty of idolatry; the men, and women who were not virgins, of the town of Jabesh-gilead were put under the *ḥerem* because that town had not taken part in the war against the Benjaminites (cf. Judges 21. 11).

Related to the *anathema* in its destructive aspect is the penalty of being "cut off from one's people" (cf. Lev. 7. 20 f., 25, 27; 17. 9; 19. 8; Num. 9. 13). This punishment, frequently invoked against Israelites who violate the Law, may originally have meant that the violator was to be put to death or outlawed. But the expression occurs in certain texts in which that meaning would be absurd, because the sin for which it is the penalty could not possibly be known to anyone but the sinner himself (cf. Lev. 7. 20 f.).

Consequently, it is probable that it denotes an invocation on the sinner of the punishment of God, with full assurance that God will execute it.[1] It is not even certain that the "people" from which the evildoer is to be cut off is the community of Israel rather than his own family; the latter is certainly the meaning of "people" in Leviticus 21. 1, 4, 14, 15, and in the similar expression "to be gathered to one's people" (cf. Gen. 25. 8; 49. 29). This suggests that in the penalty formula the meaning may be similarly restricted. It would be a dubious procedure, at best, to

[1] Cf. K. Elliger, *Leviticus* (Tübingen, 1966), p. 101.

attempt to explain ecclesiastical excommunication as a procedure in direct continuity with either the *anathema* or the penalty of being "cut off" from one's people.

Yet the Old Testament does furnish one example which is instructive for our purposes. In Ezra 10. 8, those who had returned from the Exile and who had married pagan wives are bidden to come to Jerusalem for the dissolution of their irregular marriages. The penalty for one who refused to do so was that "all his property should be forfeited and he himself banned (MT *yibbadel*; LXX *diastalēsetai*) from the congregation of the exiles". Because this example deals with a matter of discipline, it is not directly pertinent to the question of sanction for error in matters of belief, but the exclusion from the community herein envisaged is a closer parallel than any other in the Old Testament to ecclesiastical excommunication.

II. New Testament

1. *The Pauline Epistles and Matthew*

When one passes to the New Testament, one finds Paul's cursing of anyone who preaches to the Galatians a gospel different from that which they had received from him (Gal. 1. 8 f.). The "let him be *anathema*" of those verses is not precisely an excommunication formula, but a wish for the offender's extermination and damnation, similar to Romans 9. 3 (cf. also 1 Cor. 16. 22).[2] The finality and far-reaching effect of the *anathema* makes it clear that there is much dissimilarity between Paul's *anathema* and the later use of the word by the Church. It is, however, in the *anathema* of Galatians 1. 8 f., and 1 Corinthians 16. 22, that we find the closest parallel in the New Testament to ecclesiastical excommunication for *doctrinal* reasons.[3] The former text, especially, indicates that for the apostle there is such a thing as a doctrinal position which is incompatible with the faith and

[2] Cf. K. Hofmann, "Anathema", in *Reallexicon für Antike und Christentum*, 1, 429.

[3] Cf. H. Schlier, *Der Brief an die Galater* (Göttingen, [4]1965), p. 41: "... es für den Apostel eine Norm der Verkündigung gibt, eben sein Evangelium, und damit auch grundsätzlich die Möglichkeit zwischen wahrer und falscher Verkündigung zu unterscheiden".

incompatible with one's remaining in the Christian community. Doctrinal excommunication as practised by the later Church appears to be a combination of that awareness with the less radical penalty of Ezra 10. 8—the Church no longer invokes the final, destructive *anathema* of Galatians, but imposes exclusion from the Christian community upon those who, in its judgment, have repudiated the common faith.

In most cases the exclusion from the community spoken of in the Pauline epistles is far more drastic than a mere penal separation from it in this life. That is true not only of the above-mentioned texts but of the case of the incestuous man in 1 Corinthians 5. 1–13. There, a member of the community has married his stepmother. Those exegetes who refuse to regard the sin as the product of a "pneumatic antinomianism"[4] do not see it as having any *doctrinal* significance. But it is difficult not to find a connection between the Corinthians' being "puffed up" and "boasting" (cf. 1 Cor. 5. 2, 6), and a belief on their part that the incestuous man's conduct was that of a truly "spiritual" person, superior to ethical norms. In any case, one must grant that whether the fault was due to a doctrinaire pneumatism or not, the reaction of Paul is directed primarily to the moral irregularity itself. The "handing over to Satan" of the delinquent is not excommunication; something graver is involved. The purpose of the handing over is "the destruction of the flesh", in other words, the sinner's death, "so that his spirit may be saved on the day of the Lord" (1 Cor. 5. 5).

The procedure is similar to that found in the account of the deaths of Ananias and Sapphira (Acts 5. 5, 10) and in the story of the punishment of Elymas (Acts 13. 8–12), although in the latter case, and probably in the former, the one who works the calamity is not Satan but the Lord. The handing over to Satan is connected with the command, "Cast out the evil person from your midst" (1 Cor. 5. 13), a quotation from Deuteronomy, where it is used (though not invariably; cf. Deut. 19. 19) in the sense of putting a malefactor to death (cf. Deut. 17. 7; 22. 21, 24; 24. 7). Paul looks for the ultimate salvation of the sinner, but the purpose of

[4] So W. Kümmel in H. Lietzmann, *An die Korinther* I/II Tübingen, [4]1949), p. 173.

his action is not merely to save the sinner but to purify the community (cf. 1 Cor. 5. 6).[5]

While the extreme measure of "handing over to Satan" is demanded by the apostle only in the case of the incestuous man, 1 Corinthians 5. 11 shows that those guilty of certain grave sins were to be avoided by their fellow Christians; in practice, an excommunication of sorts is demanded for them too. The Christian is not to associate with them, and the command not to eat with them would include a ban on sharing the Eucharist with them even though it cannot be understood as pertaining directly, much less exclusively, to that.[6] And none of the sins mentioned has to do with errors of faith.[7]

In summary, one may say that the Pauline epistles speak of a damning curse for those who preach a perverted form of the gospel, or who do not "love the Lord Jesus". They give evidence of a handing over to Satan of a man who is a notorious sinner, and they demand avoidance of fellow Christians who have sinned in a variety of ways. In respect to exclusion from the community by a method less drastic than exclusion through death, only the last is similar to later ecclesiastical excommunication. But the similarity should not be overstretched, for avoidance of the sinners is not a formal casting-out of them from the community.

Exclusion from the community by judicial pronouncement is found in the Gospel of Matthew. In the "ecclesiastical discourse" the case is presented of a Christian who sins against his brother Christian and who refuses correction even when it is given by "the church" (Mt. 18. 17). He is to be regarded as "a heathen and a tax-collector", that is, as one who does not belong to the *ekklēsia*. But the matter in question is offence against another member of the community, not an erroneous interpretation of the faith. It is true that this verse is immediately followed by the *logion*, "Amen I say to you, whatever you bind on earth shall be

[5] Cf. W. Doskocil, "Exkommunication", in *Reallexicon für Antike und Christentum*, VII (Fasc. 49), 14. Doskocil's view that the punishment was also to atone for the sin is without basis.

[6] Cf. H. Lietzmann, *op. cit.*, p. 25.

[7] The "idolaters" of 5. 11 are a possible exception. But Paul seems to be thinking here of Christians who take part in the sacrificial banquets of the pagans (cf. 1 Cor. 10. 14–22) on the principle that the idols to whom the food was offered are nothing.

bound in heaven, and whatever you loose on earth shall be loosed in heaven" (Mt. 18. 18).

The question whether that *logion* is here directed to the *ekklēsia* as such, or only to a certain group within it, is much disputed, but that does not directly concern us here. At very least, such binding and loosing is a prerogative of the Church. But what does it pertain to? The rabbinic parallels to the *logion* suggest that it concerns both discipline and teaching.[8] While the proposing of teaching does not suit the context of Matthew 18. 18, the meaning of the *logion* as such should not be restricted to the specific instance of disciplinary action found in Matthew 18, namely, exclusion of the offender from the community (and, conversely, lifting the ban should he repent). The *logion* existed as an independent unit before its incorporation into Matthew 18, and it is found, in reference to Peter alone, in Matthew 16. 19. In the latter context, no such limitation of its meaning is given as in Matthew 18. It must be noted, however, that the rabbinic parallels, while they give evidence of binding and loosing in respect to teaching, do not afford any examples of teaching on matters of belief, but only of declaring certain moral conduct forbidden or permitted.

The similarity of Matthew 18. 15–17 with the Qumrân Manual of Discipline has often been remarked on (cf. 1QS 6, 1), although in that particular text nothing is said about exclusion from the community. However, the Manual does contain examples of exclusion, sometimes permanent (cf. 1QS 7, 23 ff.; 9, 1).

2. *The other New Testament Data*

When one comes to the Pastoral Epistles, one finds clear evidence that the separation of certain members from the community, to which some of the earlier texts bear witness, is now directed to those who have erred primarily in doctrine rather than in moral practice. It is true that in the Pastorals there is no evidence of formal excommunication of those offenders, but the avoidance of them which "Paul" counsels is tantamount to that penalty. Second Timothy 3. 5 demands that "Timothy" avoid men who are described in terms which are in large part those of a traditional catalogue of vices (cf. 2. Tim. 3. 2–4), but their distinctive

[8] Cf. H. Strack–P. Billerbeck, *Kommentar zum Neuen Testament aus Talmud und Midrasch*, 1 (München, [2]1956), pp. 738–41.

offence is that "while having the outward show of religion (*eusebeia*) they deny its power";[9] some of them lead foolish women astray by their erroneous teaching; they oppose the truth, and are perverted in mind and reprobate in respect to the faith (cf. 2 Tim. 3. 5–8).

Similarly, "Titus" is ordered to avoid a "heretic" (*hairetikon anthropon*) who declines to be corrected (Tit. 3. 10). The position attributed to Timothy and Titus as delegates of the apostle gives those commands a public character which goes beyond mere advice given to a private person. Among the heretics is a certain Hymenaeus who, together with Philetus, claims that the resurrection of the dead has already taken place, and so disturbs the faith of others (2 Tim. 2. 17 f.). Hymenaeus is also mentioned in 1 Timothy 1. 19 f. as one of those who have "made shipwreck of the faith"; the apostle has handed him and Alexander over to Satan in order that they may learn not to blaspheme.

The latter is a most important text. The "handing over to Satan", while closely related to the procedure of 1 Corinthians 5. 5, has a less drastic consequence than that. It is a corrective measure, and plainly the death of the sinners is not envisaged. The bodily evils expected to befall them as a result of the handing-over are not specified; M. Dibelius suggests "sickness or something similar".[10] Also, unlike the case of 1 Corinthians 5, it is not moral fault but doctrinal error (probably the one specified in 2 Tim. 2. 18) which has occasioned the censure. The closeness of the procedure to ecclesiastical excommunication is apparent, and the sanction has been incurred for an "interpretation of the faith" which the apostle judges to be a falsification and denial of it.

The First Epistle of John is also important for our inquiry since it deals in large part with christological error: the denial that Jesus is the Christ (1 Jn. 2. 22). Expressed positively, the true Christian is the one who confesses that Jesus is the Son of God (4. 15; 5. 5), that Jesus is the Christ (5. 1), that Jesus Christ has come in the flesh (4. 2), that Jesus Christ came by water and

[9] Cf. M. Dibelius–H. Conzelmann, *Die Pastoralbriefe* (Tübingen, [4]1966), p. 87: "Hier (in verse 5) verliert die Lasterreihe ihren traditionellen Charakter; die folgenden Worte enthalten also einen wirklichen Vorwurf gegen die Ketzer."

[10] *Ibid*., p. 28.

blood (5. 6). In this epistle, the denial that Jesus is the Christ is hardly meant as a denial that he is the Messiah. The epistle gives no evidence of being directed against Jewish beliefs but, rather, against those of people who claim the Christian name, and a denial of Jesus' messiahship by such persons is not credible. Rudolf Bultmann's reduction of the erroneous teaching to a denial that the historical Jesus is identical with the eschatological Christ, the pre-existent Saviour, is insufficient.[11] For Bultmann, such verses as 1. 7b; 2. 2, and 4. 10b, which attribute salvation to the expiatory death (the "blood") of Jesus are foreign to the thought of the author and come from an ecclesiastical redactor.[12]

But the view of Rudolf Schnackenburg is preferable: that these affirmations are valuable as an indication of what is implied in the confessional statements "Jesus is the Christ", "Jesus is the Son of God", "Jesus Christ has come in the flesh". If those confessions and all the affirmations about Jesus Christ are taken together, one has the christology of the author and, conversely, the content of the false teaching.[13] As against Bultmann,[14] Schnackenburg does not think that "Docetism" is the christological error against which the author speaks, although he admits that there are points of contact between the false teaching repudiated in the epistles and Docetism.[15] Rather, the teaching is a denial of redemption through the saving death of the historical Jesus who is also the pre-existent, heavenly Christ, the only-begotten Son of God. For Bultmann, to deny that Jesus Christ has come in the flesh is to separate the historical Jesus and the eschatological Christ; for Schnackenburg, it means to deny that the work of redemption has been wrought through Jesus Christ.[16]

The epistle emphasizes the incompatibility of this teaching with the Christian faith: the false teachers, the "antichrists" (2. 18),

[11] Cf. *Die Johannesbriefe* (Göttingen, 1967), pp. 43 f.

[12] *Ibid.*, pp. 27, 29 f., 73.

[13] Cf. *Die Johannesbriefe* (Freiburg/Basel/Wien, ^{2}1963), p. 18: "Diese volle und an keiner Stelle auftrennbare joh. Christologie setzt der Verf. den Irrlehrern entgegen.... Die Christologie ist aufs engste mit der Soteriologie verbunden."

[14] *Op. cit.*, p. 67.

[15] *Op. cit.*, p. 22: "... eine ausgesprochen 'doketische' Christologie wird nicht erkennbar".

[16] *Ibid.*, p. 19.

have gone out from the Christian community; they never really belonged to it, for if they had, they would not have gone out from it (2. 19). This "going out" does not suggest any excommunication or casting-out of the false teachers by the Church.[17] But their separation from the body of believers could not be expressed more sharply: even before their promotion of the false teaching, they were not really Christians. The impossibility of the co-existence within the Church of the true faith and the beliefs of the false teachers is most clearly brought to expression. As Bultmann points out, this repudiation of the false teachers indicates that they claimed to be Christians; to this, the author retorts that they never were. It is disputed whether their "going out" indicates a voluntary separation from the community.[18] But in any case, the author holds that their teaching has indeed separated them from the Church; to remain there one must hold the true faith. Bultmann distinguishes between the "empirical" and the "real" community, and maintains that the heretics still belonged to the former, though not to the latter.[19] For him, the epistle's constant warnings against them as a danger to the believers indicate that.

The argument is not convincing; a group which had separated, claiming that its doctrine was the true one, could still create a danger for those within the community, and be the object of the author's warnings. But whether 2. 19c means that the false teachers are still within the community, thus showing that not all who claim to belong to the real community actually do (so Bultmann), or that they have left it, thus showing that none of them ever really belonged to the Church (so Schnackenburg[20]), it is plain that the christological errors which they propound are intolerable, and that the one Church cannot accept the two differing christologies. The designation of the heretics as "antichrists" (2. 18) and "false prophets" (4. 1) is clear indication of that. Denial that Jesus is the Christ is equivalent to denial of God the Father; he who denies the Son has no share in the life of the Father (2.

[17] Cf. W. Bauer, *Rechtgläubigkeit und Ketzerei im altesten Christentum* (Tübingen, ²1964), p. 96.

[18] So Schnackenburg, *op. cit.*, p. 150; C. H. Dodd, *The Johannine Epistles* (London and New York, 1946), p. 52; *contra*, Bultmann, *op. cit.*, p. 41.

[19] *Op. cit.*, p. 42.

[20] *Op. cit.*, p. 151.

22 f.). Thus, the false teaching is the same as idolatry, and the exhortation "Little children, keep yourselves from idols" (5. 21) means that they are to keep themselves from the errors about Jesus the Christ.[21]

In 2 John an even more pronounced statement of the incompatibility between the true faith and the false teaching is found. The false teachers are designated there as "deceivers" who "have gone out into the world" (v. 7). As verse 10 indicates, the movement is spread by travelling missionaries, although it is probable that the "going out" is also intended as a reference to the "going out" from the community of which John 2. 19 speaks. Their error is formulated in terms similar to those of 1 John 4. 2: there, the error is denial that "Jesus Christ has come (*elēluthota*) in the flesh"; here, that "Jesus Christ comes (*erchomenon*) in the flesh". The difference in tense of the two Greek participles is probably not of major importance. The present may emphasize "the timeless significance of the Incarnation",[22] or, as C. H. Dodd holds, it may simply be equivalent to a statement of the reality of the Incarnation, identical in meaning with 1 John 4. 2.[23] The "deceivers" think their views "advanced" (v. 9), but for the author of the epistle, one whose doctrine is so advanced that it goes beyond "the teaching of Christ" (v. 9; the genitive is probably objective: "teaching about Christ"[24]) has no fellowship with God. The community to which the epistle is sent is warned against such teachers; should one of them come into its midst he should not be received or even greeted, for to do so would be to share in his evil works (vv. 10 f.). Advice of such character makes it clear that for the author the false teachers are indeed separated from the Christian fellowship, even though as in 1 John there is no indication of a formal excommunication.

The epistles of Jude and 2 Peter are examples of especially violent polemic and warnings against false teachers, to whom are attributed gross moral faults as well as errors which are in part christological (Jude 4; 2 Pet. 2. 1; probably also 1. 16). But these men have not separated from the Church; on the contrary, they

[21] So Bultmann, *op. cit.*, pp. 93 f.
[22] Schnackenburg, *op. cit.*, p. 313; similarly Bultmann, *op. cit.*, p. 107.
[23] *Op. cit.*, p. 149.
[24] So Bultmann, *op. cit.*, p. 108.

participate in the community meals (2 Pet. 2. 13) and in the love feasts (Jude 12).[25]

III. The More Effective Way

The scope set for this article was an investigation of the biblical data in attempting to answer the question, "If the Church thinks that she has to reject certain interpretations of the faith, should this also have to involve a sanction?" Fortunately, the determining of what interpretations of faith the Church might decide she had to reject does not lie within the scope of our task, for in the complexity of the development of doctrine and of the hermeneutical problem it is not easy to say what particular interpretations are to be rejected.

It does, however, seem reasonably clear that an interpretation which would contradict the central christological and soteriological affirmations of the New Testament, an interpretation such as those against which the author of 1 John polemicizes, would indeed be such. Undoubtedly, the New Testament has various levels of christology and soteriology. But to deny a later stage (e.g., to deny Jesus' pre-existence), and appeal to the fact that the doctrine in question was not held by early Christians of quite undoubted "orthodoxy", would be to overlook the fact that from the viewpoint of the Church which established the New Testament canon, the whole truth is represented not by any one, or by several, of the parts, but by the whole. We are perhaps too ready to assign various levels of development to the Palestinian, Hellenistic-Jewish and Hellenistic strata respectively.

But even granting the historical accuracy of that stratifying, it is difficult to see how an interpretation which in effect dissolves the christology of any of the strata into a symbol of some "higher" truth, can be regarded as an acceptable formulation of the Christian faith. But be that as it may, if the Church does decide that a particular interpretation is to be rejected, should a sanction, that is, excommunication, be attached to holding it? On

[25] For a discussion of the false teachers of these epistles and their doctrines, cf. K. Schelkle, *Die Petrusbriefe/Der Judasbrief* (Freiburg/Basel/Wien, 1961), pp. 230–4.

principle, it is impossible to say that it ought not. W. Doskocil has said, and quite amply demonstrated, that "every social group, past and present, claims for itself the right, under certain circumstances, to exclude some of its members either permanently or temporarily".[26] Historically, the Christian Church has been no exception, and its conduct has biblical warrant. A case of formal excommunication is rare in the New Testament, and it is difficult to find even one instance of excommunication for errors of faith, but it is only a slight step from the demand that Christians who have erred in faith be avoided by their fellows to formal excommunication. Is there any reason why the Church should change her conduct in this respect?

Perhaps the example of Vatican II affords an answer. There is no need to say that not all its documents deal with the faith, and even those which do, propose certain views to which a faithful Catholic can take exception. But it is equally true that such documents as the Dogmatic Constitution on the Church were meant to represent, in their totality, the Church's faith and to command the assent of believers. Yet the Council, of set purpose, did not pronounce a single *anathema*. A setting forth of the faith, such as that done by the Council, is probably in our times a more effective way than excommunication for the Church to bear witness to "the faith once for all delivered to the saints" (Jude 3).

[26] *Art. cit.*, 2.

Antonius Brekelmans

Origin and Function of Creeds in the Early Church

THE observations which constitute the body of this article can be grouped under three headings which correspond to the most obvious situations that gave rise to the various creeds and determined their function, namely, the liturgy, religious instruction and baptism, and the fight against heresy.[1] The first will be called the "creed of worship", because it is primarily used in the liturgy, particularly the Eucharist, and is part of the worship and praise of God. The other two will quite naturally be called the "baptismal creed" and the "doctrinal creed".[2]

I. The Creed of Worship

The most obvious situation where a creed was required was the liturgical celebration. This was not a matter of external circumstances which challenged the individual believer or the community to state their belief, but an inner religious need to praise and thank God for the gift of salvation.

A number of psalms, and the so-called *Šema*, served already as a kind of creed in the worship of the Old Testament and late Judaism, and these undoubtedly had some influence on the liturgy

[1] See O. Cullmann, *La foi et le culte de l'Eglise primitive* (Neuchâtel, 1963), pp. 56–66.

[2] The principal creeds can be found in Denzinger–Schönmetzer, *Enchiridion Symbolorum* ([32]1963, or in older editions). The most important study of them is that by J. N. D. Kelly, *Early Christian Creeds* (London, [2]1960).

of the early Christians. In the epistles of Paul and John's Book of Revelation, we find hymns or fragments which according to biblical experts originated in the earliest Christian liturgy. The need to confess found particular expression in singing. An unknown author mentioned by Eusebius (d. 339) in his *Ecclesiastical History*[3] says: "Who does not know . . . the many psalms and songs, written by our brothers in the faith since the earliest beginnings, which celebrate the Word of God, the Christ, and look on him as God?" Unfortunately only a few liturgical hymns of the second and third centuries have come down to us, and even then most of these originated in gnostic circles.[4] Apart from this, we also know that, next to the hymns, Old Testament psalms, interpreted christologically, had a place in the liturgy.[5]

It is noteworthy that in the early Christian liturgy there was plenty of room for improvisation (cf. 1 Cor. 14. 26). This was also the case for the anaphora (the Canon of the Mass). Thus Justin wrote in 150–55: "The president offers prayers and thanksgiving according to his ability to which the people reply, 'Amen!' "[6] And when, about 215, Hippolytus wrote an example of an anaphora for the Church of Rome, he said explicitly: "The bishop says grace according to what we have said above. It is, however, not in the least necessary for him to use the same words, so that he has to take the trouble . . . to learn them by heart. Each may pray as it suits him. It is fine if somebody can make up a long and noble prayer, but when somebody prays and uses a definite prayer, he should not be prevented, as long as his prayer is irreproachable and orthodox."[7] We should not be astonished at the freedom left to improvisation since the creed of worship is the most direct and spontaneous expression of a living faith.

It is impossible to give in this short article the whole development of hymns, prayers and anaphorae in detail. We therefore

[3] *Hist. Eccl.*, v, 28, 5.

[4] See J. Quasten, *Patrology I: The Beginnings of Patristic Literature* (Utrecht/Brussels, 1950), pp. 158–68.

[5] See B. Fischer, *Die Psalmenfrömmigkeit der Märtyrerkirche* (Freiburg im Breisgau, 1949).

[6] *Apologia*, 1, 67, 5 (*P.G.* 6, c. 429).

[7] *Traditio Apostolica*, 10.

concentrate on the doxologies.[8] They constitute a kind of crystallization of the creed expressed in worship. The doxology is the most striking expression of the inner structure of Christian prayer. The formula has had an interesting development which reflects the awareness of the mystery of the Trinity. With Paul, the earliest Church prayed: "To him, therefore, who alone is wisdom, give glory through Jesus Christ for ever and ever. Amen" (Rom. 16. 27; cf. 1. 8; 7. 25; 2 Cor. 1. 20; Heb. 13. 15; 1 Pet. 4. 11).

We see the first phase of this development in the middle of the second century when the Holy Spirit, too, is drawn into mediation. Thus Justin says: "[The president] ... offers honour and praise to the Father of all through the name of the Son and of the Holy Spirit."[9] While many doxologies which only mention the mediation of Christ continue to be used, we notice a step further in this development with the Apostolic Tradition of Hippolytus who lays down that "Every blessing must end with the words: Glory to thee, Father and Son with the Holy Spirit in the Church now and always and for ever and ever. Amen."[10]

The novelty consists in that both the Son and the Holy Spirit are put on a level with the Father. The mention of the Church in the doxology just quoted is a significant addition by Hippolytus himself. For the Church is the liturgical community where people confess in this liturgical way. In Egypt we have Dionysius of Alexandria who ends a letter with the same doxology: "... we end with the example and norm handed on to us by the presbyters before us, and as we pray in conformity with them so we have now conveyed this manner of praying to you: Glory and power be to God the Father and the Son our Lord Jesus Christ with the Holy Spirit. ..."[11] Elsewhere in the East, apart from Syria, the most frequently used doxology was: "Glory to the Father through the Son in the Holy Spirit. ..." When we try to

[8] An outline of the development can be found in A. Stuiber, "Doxologie", in *Reallexikon f. Antike u. Christentum*, II, pp. 210–26.

[9] *Apologia*, I, 65, 3 (*P.G.* 6, c. 428).

[10] 6, *loc. cit.*, 36; cf. *ibid.*, 4, *loc. cit.* 33; 22, *loc. cit.*, 52.

[11] C. L. Feltoe, *The Letters and Remains of Dionysius of Alexandria* (Cambridge Patristic Texts, Cambridge, 1904), p. 198; cf. G. Kretschmar, *Studien zur frühchristlichen Trinitätstheologie* (Beitr. zur Hist. Theol., 21, Tübingen, 1956), pp. 182–3.

find out the causes which determined this development in the second and third centuries, the answer is most probably that these doxologies underwent the influence of the trinitarian baptismal formulas which were prompted by the theological controversies of the time. This seems to be indicated by a statement of Hippolytus in his fight against the monarchians or modalists: "[Because the Logos] did not want the Father to be glorified in any other way than this, he charged his disciples after the resurrection: Go and make all nations my disciples by baptizing them in the name of the Father, the Son and the Holy Spirit. He thus made it clear that anyone who excludes even one of these three, does not glorify God perfectly."[12] The Arian controversy stimulated this trend in the fourth and fifth centuries.[13] This led to the explicit trinitarian doxology: "Glory to the Father, the Son and the Holy Spirit."

It is remarkable that the earlier doxologies continued to be used in most liturgies. This may be explained by the fact that the local churches enjoyed a large measure of autonomy and that they only needed to cope with their immediate concrete situation. But this continuity also shows that the *lex orandi* (the law of prayer) guaranteed an orthodox understanding of the faith.

II. The Baptismal Creed

In order to understand the origin and structure of the baptismal creed, we must make a distinction, based on the later ritual of baptism, between (*a*) the baptismal formula pronounced by him who administers baptism, (*b*) the questions put to the candidate for baptism, and (*c*) the answers he gives.

Regarding the baptismal formula, we take for granted that in the early Church the name of Christ was pronounced over the candidate. This may be deduced from the data of the New Testament where people are said to be baptized "in" or "unto the name of Christ". Thus the Epistle of James mentions: "the good name invoked over you" (2. 7). About the middle of the second

[12] *Fragm. contra Noetum*, 14. Cf. P. Nautin, *Hippolyte, Contre les hérésies; fragment, étude et édition critique* (Paris, 1949), p. 255.

[13] Cf. J. A. Jungmann, *Die Stellung Christi im liturgischen Gebet* (Liturgiegesch. Quellen u. Forsch. 19/20, Münster im Westphalia, 1925).

century Hermas speaks of those who succumbed to the persecutions and became apostates as those "who were ashamed of the name invoked over them".[14] This is without doubt the name of Christ, after whom the believers were called "Christians". Side by side with this formula we know that the formula "in the name of the Father, the Son and the holy Spirit" (Matt. 28. 19) also existed. It was mentioned in the *Didachè* in the beginning of the second century.[15] Since the Jews already believed in the one God and were also acquainted with the idea of the Holy Spirit (cf. Acts 2. 14–41), it was probably enough for the early Church to baptize these Jews "in the name of Christ". On the other hand, the preaching of the gospel among the pagans required the express mention of the Father and the Spirit, which is reflected in the trinitarian formula for baptism. These two formulas do not contradict each other because they imply one and the same event of salvation.

The most important question here is whether a creed was used in baptism which took the form of question and answer. The New Testament definitely gives us the impression, at least by implication, that this form was indeed made use of. We find an illustration of it in the interpolated but old text of Acts 8. 36–8, where Philip says to the Ethiopian: "If you believe with all your heart, you may" (baptismal question). "And he replied: 'I believe that Jesus Christ is the Son of God' " (baptismal answer).[16] Lack of evidence makes it impossible to say much more about the concrete form of the question and answer procedure until we reach the middle of the second century.

From the second half of the second century on we have texts from Tertullian, Hippolytus of Rome, Dionysius of Alexandria, and Origen. Here we quote Hippolytus. The bishop, who administers baptism, asks:

"Do you believe in God, the almighty Father?"

"Do you believe in Christ Jesus, the Son of God, born of the Virgin Mary through the Holy Spirit, who was crucified under

[14] *Pastor Hermae*, Sim., VIII, 6, 4 (72).

[15] *Didachè*, 7. 1 (*Die Apostolischen Väter*, ed. Funk and Bihlmeyer, I, Tübingen, [2]1956), p. 5.

[16] See O. Cullmann, *op. cit.*, p. 57. For other examples, see Kelly, *op cit.*, pp. 29–37.

Pontius Pilate, died and was buried, rose again alive from among the dead, ascended into heaven, is seated at the right hand of the Father and will come to judge the living and the dead?"

"Do you believe in the Holy Spirit, the holy Church and the resurrection of the flesh?"[17]

This form replaced and contained the trinitarian baptismal formula. This remained the usual form in the Western Church till in the sixth century. The same probably holds also for the fourth and fifth centuries in the Eastern Church, but from John Chrysostom and Theodore of Mopsuestia we learn that about 400 this baptismal confession was linked with the renouncement of the devil.

After each of the three questions the candidate said: "I believe", and was then immersed in the water. It seems to me that these baptismal questions were not simply put to inquire whether the candidate really believed and accepted Christian teaching. They were rather meant to express the public and official offer of the reality of salvation which is present in the Church. The acceptance of it is the real "confession". Thus the form of question and answer aims at a consent, an agreement, in faith. If we do not look on this as a dead form of words but as a living and actual confession, we may say that the baptismal confession here is essentially a dialogue which tends towards agreement in faith.

Tertullian rightly describes this agreement as a *pactio fidei* (pact of faith) and a *fidei conventio* (agreement of faith).[18] The word *"symbolum"* used for the creed points in the same direction. For it was the custom in antiquity to break a coin or a ring in two to signify that an agreement had the validity of a contract. When, later on, the contract had to be proved, it was done by showing that the two pieces fitted together (*symballein*). It is reasonable to suppose that the Christians of the early Church gave the name of *"symbolum"* to their baptismal confession of faith because of this popular custom. The term appears for the first time in Cyprian who used it to signify the baptismal questions, which cannot be separated from the answers.[19] It is also

[17] *Trad. Apost.*, 21, *loc. cit.* 50–1.

[18] *De pudicitia*, 9. 16; *De anima*, 35. 3; cf. E. Dekkers, *Tertullianus en de geschiedenis van de liturgie* (Brussels, 1947), pp. 195–6.

[19] *Ep.* 69, 7. 1 (*Saint Cyprien, Correspondance*, II, ed. Bayard, Paris, [2]1961, p. 244); cf. *Ep.* 75, 11. 1 (Firmilian of Caesarea), *ibid.*, p. 298.

quite possible that the Greek word for confession, *homologia*, preserved its original profane meaning, "agreement".[20]

III. The Doctrinal Creed

By "doctrinal creed", traditionally called the *symbolum fidei*, we understand a concise formulation of the teaching of faith, which may claim a certain completeness. Such a creed has its origin and function in the framework of religious instruction, apologetics and the fight against heresy.

The New Testament and Apostolic Fathers only contain doctrinal statements, which may be considered fragments and initial formulas of doctrinal creeds in the light of later developments.[21] Examples of a concise summary of doctrine can be found about 200 in Irenaeus and Tertullian, when they write about the rule of faith, or of truth. This very phrase shows that it is meant to be a faithful summary of the traditional teaching. According to Irenaeus this rule must contain the following points: "... belief in one God, the almighty Father, who has created heaven and earth and the sea and all that is contained therein; and in one Jesus Christ, the Son of God, who has become man for our salvation; and in the Holy Spirit who, through the prophets, announced the works of salvation (*oikonomias*), the coming, the virgin birth, the suffering, the resurrection from the dead and the bodily ascension of the beloved Jesus Christ, our Lord, and his return from heaven in the glory of the Father in order to restore all things and to raise all human flesh to life".[22]

"To this Irenaeus adds that in this way he transmits the religious teaching which has been handed down from the apostles and which the churches all over the world have in common. It was very much in his interest to stress both the apostolic origin and the universality of the doctrine since he fought the gnostic heresies on the basis of these two arguments. If he had based his

[20] See J. Ratzinger, *Einführung in das Christentum. Vorlesungen über das Apostolische Glaubensbekenntnis* (Munich, 1968), pp. 61–9.

[21] Cf. D. Van Den Eynde, *Les normes de l'enseignement chrétien dans la littérature patristique des trois premiers siècles* (Gembloux/Paris, 1933), pp. 281–313.

[22] *Adv. Haer.*, 1, 10. 1 (Harvey, 1, 90).

arguments only on tradition, supported by the apostolic succession, this would not be adequate as a criterion of orthodoxy. The universality of the teaching is therefore essential: "[The Church] believes unanimously, as with one soul and one heart, and transmits it [*kerygma* and doctrine] as if she spoke with one mouth. There are, no doubt, different languages, spread over the face of the earth, but the power of tradition is one and the same. Churches established in Germania do not believe nor transmit this belief differently, nor the Churches established in Iberia, nor those of the Celts, nor those in the East, nor those in Egypt. . . ."[23] It should be noted that when Irenaeus speaks of tradition he means the actual transmission of the religious teaching. Thus the rule of faith consists of those elements which are transmitted, taught and believed universally. According to him it is possible for heretics to have the same kind of formulation but because they are outside the Church they have a different understanding of the faith.[24]

The examples of a rule of faith which we find in Irenaeus and Tertullian show that, while the content is fixed, the formulation is still relatively free, and this content embraces the fundamental elements of religious doctrine. Among these the statements about Christ begin to predominate. They continue the christological tradition which originated in the apostolic *kerygma* and can be clearly seen in the letters of Ignatius of Antioch, the writings of Justin and also in the baptismal questions.

As we have these rules of faith now, we can see that they were composed and used as weapons in the fight against heresy. Nevertheless, this was probably not their only function. Irenaeus, for instance, speaks of the Christian "who received the rule of truth at baptism and retained it without change".[25] Although the phrase "rule of faith" primarily refers to the fixed content of the teaching of the faith, one can take it, with Kelly,[26] that similar summaries were also used in catechetics. It seems obvious that the catechist needed such a concise formulation. The catechetical rules of faith—or whatever name we give them—by their nature

[23] *Adv. Haer.*, I, 10. 2 (Harvey, I, 126).
[24] Cf. Van Den Eynde, *op. cit.*, p. 288.
[25] *Adv. Haer.*, I, 20 (Harvey, I, 88).
[26] Kelly, *Early Christian Creeds*, pp. 49–52.

aim at baptism, and are, no doubt, based on the baptismal formula and the baptismal questions.[27] This would explain the trinitarian division of these rules of faith and of the later creeds (*symbola fidei*). When we ask which of the two types of rule, the catechetical or the anti-heretical, was first in the field, the catechetical was certainly the first. This does not mean, however, that these catechetical rules were also influenced by the fight against heresy.

When, in the fourth century, the catechumenate had become an organized institution, the function of the rules of faith was taken over by the creeds (*symbola fidei*). These were based on both the rule of faith and the baptismal questions. In so far as they played their part in catechizing, we might call them catechetical doctrinal creeds, but they should not be confused with the baptismal questions. Such a creed was transmitted by the bishop to the catechumen three weeks before baptism in a liturgical function (*traditio symboli*). As head and representative of the local Church, the bishop officially communicated the Church's teaching to the new Christian. The articles of faith were explained during the following two weeks, and this was followed by the "handing back" (*redditio*) of the creed, which meant that the candidate had to recite it by heart.[28] Thus in the fourth century every Church had a broadly uniform creed which clearly had a doctrinal function. This creed was formulated in the light of the proper baptismal creed. The relation between the two may be roughly described as that between the "faith which is believed" (*fides quae*) and the "faith by which we believe" (*fides qua creditur*).

Finally, there is still another type of doctrinal creed, the conciliar or anti-heretical creed or *symbolum*. The older conciliar creeds are always based on the catechetical creed. This shows, on the one hand, that the anti-heretical creed was intended to maintain the transmitted doctrine, and on the other, that it was also intended to fill the urgent need to combat heresy. It is typical of this type of creed that the formulation or terminology begins to operate as the general norm for the true teaching of the faith. A clear example in the Nicaean creed which used the term

[27] Cf. Van Den Eynde, *op. cit.*, p. 312, and A. Benoît, *Saint Irénée. Introduction à l'étude de sa théologie* (Paris, 1960), p. 208.
[28] See Kelly, *op. cit.*, pp. 32–40.

"homo-ousios" (of the same substance); this term became the touchstone of orthodoxy in the theological controversy which broke out after the council.[29] It would appear that to defend orthodoxy with mere terminology was not exactly a happy choice, at least in the fight against Arianism. In actual fact, the Nicaean creed was only accepted as a norm of the faith when agreement had been reached about its content.

In conclusion we refer to the three main types of creed. The creed of worship is the most direct and spontaneous expression of the living faith. The baptismal creed expresses the dialogue between catechumen and Church, tending towards an "agreement". In the doctrinal creeds we have to distinguish between the anti-heretical or conciliar creed and the catechetical creed. The first is meant to be the norm of faith, while the second communicates the doctrine of faith and aims at the baptismal creed.

[29] Denz.-Schönm., n. 125 (54). See Kelly, *op. cit.*, pp. 205-62.

Translated by Theo Westow

Engelbert Gutwenger

The Role of the Magisterium

I AM concerned not with the *magisterium*'s *de facto* role, but with the one that belongs to it *de jure*. That the distinction can be made, at least implies that the Church's teaching authority has been set quite clear limits, and that these are not always observed. The whole situation is very confused and grows worse rather than better. It is theology's task to unravel it as objectively and honestly as it can. Were we to find that the *magisterium* has overreached itself, then it would be better to put it in its proper place, for this would necessarily involve the salutary clarification of its real rights within its own field.

The origin of the present unrest lies in part in the historical decline that stretches from a time in which authority was able to do more or less as it pleased, to the modern age in which such absolutism is unacceptable to a society that in the meanwhile has become educated and articulate. Any reasonable man will concede that for as long as the Church consisted largely of illiterates, its teaching authority was rightly granted wide scope when giving guidance in the faith, and in morals particularly. But what was then regarded as guidance is felt by modern man to be regimentation. As is well known, ecclesiastical authority in every era has acted in a spirit similar to that shown by the secular authorities dominant at the time. For as long as these were not democracies, there was no apparent conflict; but now that so many of them are, it is important to examine the workings of ecclesiastical authority in order to see what is still valid and what, as the products of environmental influences, should be left behind.

I. The Sociological Approach

Ecclesiastical authority has three aspects: *potestas regendi*, *potestas sanctificandi* and *potestas docendi*. As regards the *potestas docendi* in general, one first has to decide from which angle it is to be approached, and according to what yardstick the scope of its competence is to be measured.

Clearly unacceptable is the attitude that once characterized the theological approach to this question. Starting from the major premise: "Whatever the Church authorities teach, in particular whatever the pope teaches, is true", it continued with the minor premise: "But ecclesiastical authority, in practice and theory, has said the following about its teaching rights...." This sort of reasoning overlooks the fact that it begins by adducing as true something that has yet to be shown to be so. The unspecified range and content of the major premise begs too many questions to make it acceptable.

Neither shall we get very far through appealing to tradition. To maintain that what ecclesiastical authority teaches is right today because it is doing no more than it did in the past, leaves out of account the possibility that former practice was introduced without adequate theological support. Furthermore, the argument from precedent is invalid in this case because the right to make binding decisions in the matter of truth and untruth cannot be acquired by prescription but must be adduced from other sources. Authority unearths truth; it does not make it.

But it still remains to be established in detail precisely what truth it is concerned with, when it is able to build upon infallible divine guidance, and where it must take into account the possibility of human error and work within purely human limitations. Glib appeals to tradition do not settle questions of this sort, if only because the notion of tradition cannot be used with adequate precision.

With an eye to the subsequent references to tradition in this article, it might be best to clarify our understanding of the term in this context at the outset. In Vatican II's Constitution on Divine Revelation (6, §24) it is stated that: "Sacred theology rests on the written word of God, together with sacred tradition, as its primary and perpetual foundation."[1] Further light is thrown on this statement in Chapter 6, §21, where we read that the Church has always seen the Scriptures, together with tradition, as the *suprema regula fidei.*

A comparison of the various passages that mention Scripture and tradition, and an examination of subsequent statements in the same Constitution, show that tradition is regarded as the normative interpretation of Scripture. This is also Karl Rahner's assessment of these texts: "What it is intended to say is limited by the 'together with tradition', a formula that can only be reconciled with Chapter II if tradition is understood as the still living and normative interpretation of Scripture. This intention is maintained to the extent that in what follows the references are to Scripture alone."[2]

Our concern is not with the difficulties that arise when one attempts to examine in detail the Church's normative understanding of Scripture. The point here is that Vatican II saw Scripture, rather than a theological system, as the basis of theology, even if Scripture does have to be read in accordance with the Church's living tradition, whatever that might mean in any particular case. But one has only to recall that in the patristic period the normative understanding of Scripture attributed literal value to the stories of creation, paradise, Jonah and the Whale, and the events reported by the evangelists, to see what difficulties lie concealed. One is therefore led to the conclusion that Scripture itself, as presented to us according to strict hermeneutical methods, must be normative for the Church's understanding of Scripture. Inasmuch as hermeneutics achieves progressive clarification of certain issues, there is necessarily a corresponding change in the Church's understanding of Scripture. It is not surprising, therefore, that the insertion of "tradition" in the conciliar texts quoted was not welcomed by all theologians.

Given all this, it might be thought more appropriate to approach the question of the Church's teaching authority from the point of view of its basis in Scripture, and each time a material

[1] K. Rahner and H. Vorgrimler, *Kleines Konzilskompendium* (Freiburg, 1966), p. 380.
[2] *Id.*, pp. 365 ff.

refinement of it occurred, to see what justification it had. But the yield would be minimal if we were to stick exclusively to what we can find in the Bible. It is well known that the community structures we read of in the New Testament look very crude beside the institutional structures of the modern Church. The monarchical episcopate was a relatively late arrival, and the early Church knew no such thing as a pope in our modern sense. It must also be remembered that many of the words attributed to Jesus, and which earlier ecclesiology used to justify the structures of the modern Church, are of doubtful authenticity. But even if one did wish to regard everything Jesus said as historically authentic, one could still legitimately ask if more has not been read into the texts than their literal sense could bear. On all the available biblical evidence, it is difficult to say much more than that though Jesus wanted to build a community, he left open the question of the concrete structures that would form it. The popular procedure of reading into the New Testament texts the structures we now have—the opposite, in other words, of exegesis—may well be understandable from the apologetic viewpoint, but it is scientifically unacceptable.

Much more could be achieved through a sociological approach. As a community desired by Christ, the Church possessed potential if not actual social structures from the beginning. Potential social structures subsequently activated and realized in response to historical needs can be regarded as *de iure divino.*

Authority is one of the structures that constitute a community. As the community grows in size, so authority becomes a more prominent force. The form it takes will be in part determined by the mood of the age. The hierarchical divisions within the priesthood of late Judaism may well have served as the initial model. But thereafter, the authority structures of the secular world were undoubtedly at the back of the progressive establishment of papal and episcopal power. The Church's development is to be explained not simply in terms of impulses from inside, but also in terms of its encounter with the world at large.

It is inevitable that a teaching role will develop in a human community held together by common faith. The propagation and preservation of the gospel, the gradual growth of the communities to maturity, and the confrontation with a world often hostile to their aims, gave rise to the need for other teachers in addition to the apostles. As the Church continued its outward growth, functions that had originally been exercised by apostles, their disciples, presbyters, and other charismatically gifted members of the community, became institutionalized. In all this, the formation of the teaching office and its hierarchical connections showed a constant and logical growth.

From the sociological viewpoint, it is natural enough that a Church growing in size and complexity should sooner or later give rise to an organized and professional teaching office. Its functions would include that of determining the language in which faith was to be confessed, as well as that of proclaiming the gospel.

Perhaps what I am saying could be clarified by taking an example from the secular sphere. In a nomadic tribe, laws that may well be simple and obvious nevertheless have full weight behind them. They are known by every adult member of the tribe. Their interpretation, however primitive it might be, is the result of collective thought. In comparison, the State is, of course, a much more complex organization. Functions are more numerous and varied and so are shared among various professionally competent groups. Thus, instead of a situation in which the meaning of the law is determined by the community, we have one in which this function now devolves upon the senior court. Its function is to provide a detailed, objective and precise rendering of the principles at stake.

A similar development can be observed within a religious community as it grows in complexity. At the outset, the original corpus of belief is preserved and handed on by the community almost word for word. Clarifications that may become necessary are agreed on by the community as a whole in the interests of a finer and deeper group understanding of its original possession. As the primary bearer of the faith is the ecclesial community as such (*subiectum primarium fidei*), this is right and proper. And when a papal or episcopal ministry of teaching does arise, its relationship to the faith is that of a servant charged to preserve and propagate it. (The presbyter's function in this respect is to act as representative of the bishop who by virtue of his office is the ultimate teaching authority in his diocese.) Those familiar with historical and sociological inquiry will accept this presentation of the situation because they know that development means progressive differentiation.

II. The Authentic Teaching Office and its Limits

"Magisterium" is a collective term that embraces first of all the infallible teaching office of the councils and the popes. We also speak of the *magisterium ordinarium* and mean by it the faith proclaimed by the universal episcopate. In a position on its own is the *magisterium authenticum*, which includes the non-infallible but nevertheless official instructions issued by the pope to the universal Church. These usually take the form of encyclicals. The limits within which the *magisterium authenticum* operates are not unequivocally established, as some theologians consider papal speeches, and papal letters to individual bishops and cardinals subsequently printed in *Acta Apostolicae Sedis*, to be statements of the *magisterium authenticum*. In this respect, it should at least be possible to agree that the existence of argument as to whether or not the pope used, or wished to use, the *magisterium authenticum* is of itself sufficient reason for giving him the benefit of the doubt. In strict terms, the *magisterium authenticum* operates only when the form a given statement possesses makes it clear that it is dealing with a matter of doctrine that concerns the whole Church.

Over and above this, the teaching authority of the pope can be, and is, delegated to particular institutions (e.g., the Pontifical Biblical Commission, or the Congregation of the Faith—the former Holy Office) which in earlier times exerted considerable influence on exegesis, dogmatic theology and the teaching of the faith. Nowadays, most decrees issued by the Biblical Commission are superfluous. At one time, for instance, it was presenting what it saw as Matthew's primacy over Mark as a standpoint binding on Catholics, even though the matter is of purely historical import and as such irrelevant both to faith and morals. Nevertheless, it is an instance, perhaps, of the way in which competence can be exceeded.

Similar comments could be made about the activities of the

Holy Office. Though the Holy Office was only a sort of watch-dog and had no power to issue statements concerning the nature and content of belief, it was through its influence that theological opinions lacking clear connection with revelation could be protected, and it was also responsible for the punishment of dissenting theologians, with the result that it was able to support conclusions it favoured (such as that Christ enjoyed the beatific vision while on earth) by silencing the opposition.

It must be clear by now that determining the precise scope and competence of the Church's teaching authority is no easy matter. The question of infallibility in relation to the teaching office will be treated in the next section. The point I wish to make here is that the *magisterium* has concerned itself with historical questions, exegetical questions and with opinions held by the various theological schools. By refining its methods, exegesis progresses to new insights, and in contrast to the truths of revelation, theological opinion can be set aside. It cannot be sufficiently stressed that the yardstick of faith is divine revelation together with such conclusions as can be drawn from two revealed truths. St Thomas Aquinas's comment is apposite: *actus credentis non terminatur ad enuntiabile, sed ad rem.*[3] Where the premises arising from natural knowledge are the product of a philosophy that is not watertight at every point, appeals are readily made to tradition, the word being understood here in the wide sense as the body of transmitted custom, doctrines and disciplinary regulations that originated in popular piety or theological speculation, and that are neither contained in Scripture nor contradict it.

III. Infallible Teaching Office

In comparison to what is open to him in the exercise of his authentic teaching role, the pope's use of his infallible teaching office is restricted. According to Vatican I's definition: "When he [the pope] speaks *ex cathedra*, that is, when acting in his office of pastor and teacher of all Christians, by his supreme Apostolic authority, he defines a doctrine concerning faith or

[3] II–II, *q.* 7, *a.* 2, *ad.* 2.

morals to be held by the whole Church, through the divine assistance promised him in blessed Peter, he enjoys that infallibility with which the divine redeemer willed his Church to be endowed in defining doctrine concerning faith or morals; and therefore such definitions of the said Roman Pontiff are irreformable of themselves, and not from the consent of the Church."[4]

It is of particular importance here that papal infallibility is related to the infallibility of the Church. It does not exist for its own sake but to serve the Church. The infallibility of the Church, too, is called *indefectibilitas*. A study of the relevant Vatican I documents also shows that the *indefectibilitas* is regarded as identical with the preservation of the *depositum fidei*: in other words, the Church remains basically the same throughout history because the *depositum fidei* is preserved unchanged. Papal infallibility is therefore directed towards the preservation of the *depositum fidei*. Vatican I also maintained that by the *depositum fidei* we should understand the word of God *scriptum vel traditum*. Vatican II hoped to lessen the embarrassment caused by the *vel traditum* by explaining that tradition is simply the normative interpretation of Scripture. This point I have already dealt with.

One can summarize by saying that the *depositum fidei* consists of the Church's interpretation of Scripture—where, of course, one first thinks of Christ's New Testament revelation. This is in accordance with Christ's demand: "Teach them to believe what I have told you." The notion recurs in St John's account of Christ's last discourse with his disciples, where he says that the Spirit will remind them of what he has told them, and will help them to understand it. (The Old Testament, also, is important to Christians, because of the value Christ placed on it.)

Though the participants at Vatican I were in possession of a complete outline of a Constitution on the Church, the outbreak of the Franco-German war in 1870 brought their deliberations to a premature end. Only four of the fifteen chapters had received final attention. It is interesting that Kleutgen, who introduced the last improved outline, made the following suggestion: "Although the Church's teaching office is essentially and primarily

[4] Const. de Ecclesiae Christi, c. 4; DS 3074.

concerned with God's word *scriptum et traditum*, it ought to be concerned with everything, for if it is not, and therefore in some cases is not empowered to make a decision, it would not be able to carry out its duty of preserving the deposit of faith."[5] Aside from this clear affirmation that the Church's teaching office is always subject to the word of God, Kleutgen is also saying that the condemnation of false doctrines and the provision of authentic interpretations is justifiable only in relation to the protection of the deposit of faith. If the teaching office wants to make a judgment that is in some other interest, it can command respect only on the basis of the arguments it proffers.

In this context, a second point in connection with Vatican I's definition of papal infallibility should be mentioned, namely the role of infallibility in the settlement of moral questions. As infallibility is directly related to the *depositum fidei*, it is evident that an infallible judgment on a matter of morals can only be pronounced where in one way or another the judgment is anticipated by that deposit. In short, an infallible definition is possible only where its object is already a datum of revelation.

All this is in accordance with the contemporary view that only those definitions are *de fide divina et catholica* whose object is a part of the deposit of faith. It is also interesting that Vatican I was not concerned to include canonizations and *facta dogmatica* in the schema on infallibility. As the connected problems were not yet sufficiently developed, it was left for the theologians to clarify them further.

IV. Invitation to Dialogue

The pope's authentic teaching office has the following attributes:

1. It can and does operate within a wider field than the infallible teaching office. For example, as the highest teaching authority, the pope interprets the natural law for the benefit of God's people. This is required of the pope in as far as to observe the natural law is a part of Christian life.

2. The *magisterium authenticum* has no claim to infallibility.

[5] M 53, 313C.

It should be noted here that when the pope does not, or for some reason cannot, speak *ex cathedra*, the possibility of error on his part cannot be ruled out. At this point, everything hinges on the arguments he puts forward in support of his conclusions. If his arguments are conclusive, then it follows that his teaching should be accepted. If, on the other hand, the pope's arguments can be refuted by other and better ones, then what he has said is of no account. Further, if in support of his viewpoint, the pope can present only partial justification in a situation where equally weighty but also equally inconclusive counter-arguments can also be adduced, then the individual can decide for himself either way, if the matter at stake is a question of morals.

This point of view is disputed by those who would say that papal authority is sufficient to render certain what would otherwise remain only a matter of probability. This viewpoint seems difficult to support, for when the truth of a particular argument is in question, authority can only then be introduced as the deciding factor when certainty is thereby established. Yet that is precisely what the pope refrains from doing when the particular form of his pronouncement shows that he has not chosen to exercise his infallible teaching office. Neither in this situation does an appeal to the Holy Spirit carry conviction. To invoke the Spirit while at the same time implicitly admitting that the appeal is probably pointless—the *magisterium authenticum* is anyway admitted to be open to error—won't do. Logic and honesty suggest that statements of the *magisterium authenticum* are ultimately invitations to a dialogue in which the pros and cons can be sorted out.

That the *magisterium authenticum* declares itself at all in a particular matter means that it is not settled once and for all. Perhaps this statement could be further clarified by an additional consideration. An act of faith is defined as the acceptance of a revealed truth because of the authority of God who revealed it. As early as the Middle Ages, scholastics had concerned themselves with the question of divine authority as the basis of faith. As every theologian knows, William of Paris maintained that the divine authority meant God's claim to absolute dominion (*supremum dominium Dei*). By virtue of this claim, God could command intellectual assent and subjection from his creatures.

But William of Paris's view found no support. Most theologians preferred to believe that God's authority was to be found in his unerring knowledge and truthfulness. Justification for this view was found in the argument that the intellect seeks truth, and is therefore attracted only by insight into God's knowledge and truthfulness. If God's creatures affirm his word by virtue of its truth rather than by virtue of his claim to absolute dominion, it is difficult to see why the situation should be different in the case of the authentic teaching office. The *magisterium authenticum* cannot of itself attract assent for the simple reason that it operates fallibly. As the authentic *magisterium*'s claim to truth is not convincing of itself, those whom it addresses have to examine the reasons the pope adduces in support of his conclusions. As I have already said, these may be convincing or unconvincing: only in the former case can they command internal assent.

In the case of natural law, certitude is not always possible, a fact that might well lead us to conclude that God wants each of us to make his own conscientious decision. What we know about natural law derives primarily from our experience of social life. The next stage is a refinement of this knowledge through philosophical speculation. The conclusions reached through this combination of direct observation and philosophical investigation are naturally found more convincing than conclusions arrived at through philosophical speculation alone, for where theories are unsupported by, or even unrelated to, experience, a measure of scepticism is likely to linger.

V. The Episcopal Teaching Office

At this point something should be said about the ordinary *magisterium*. The primary duty of the college of bishops, in union with the Bishop of Rome, is to witness to the gospel. Infallibility, or indefectibility, pertains to the ordinary *magisterium* in so far as the universal episcopate proclaims something to be a binding and irreformable truth of faith. Anything that is not directly connected to the deposit of faith is in itself reformable, even when it is proclaimed by the ordinary *magisterium*. This applies particularly to ethical questions: their history shows a degree of relativity that makes this inevitable (reference was made earlier to the doctrine that those of other confessions were entitled neither to tolerance nor to the unhindered display of their religious convictions. It was considered permissible to torture and burn them. We have come a long way since then).

The primary role of the diocesan bishop is to bear witness to the gospel, and in the exercise of this role he shares in the ordinary *magisterium*. For the rest, his teaching office is analogous to the authentic teaching office of the pope, though restricted to within the confines of his diocese. The norms that otherwise apply to the *magisterium authenticum* are, *mutatis mutandis*, applicable also to official rulings made by a diocesan bishop.

VI. The Freedom of the Theologian

Whereas some bishops have understood the signs of the times, and exercise their office in the interests of necessary growth, others feel that fidelity to their conception of the Church obliges them to maintain a conservative position. It is because of this latter group in particular that the question of freedom for theology occurs, as some of them have used repressive methods against theologians. Theologians themselves must bear some of the blame for the restrictions that have been placed on them, as they will insist on publishing in popular newspapers or in public lectures statements that still await clarification, a procedure that spreads confusion in the popular mind. The ideal would be for theologians to confine the airing of their controversial opinions to the specialized journals and to discussions with their colleagues. In those cases where the appropriate authority considers wider publication inadvisable, it can make this known and prohibit mention of the issues in question in pulpit and classroom. The real question is not so much this, but rather whether authority should silence a theologian or a discussion *tout court*, that is, forbid mention of a topic even among the theologically competent. The answer to this question should take account of the following:

1. Teaching office and theology operate at two different levels of language. The teaching office is concerned with proclaiming objective truths by witnessing to the gospel. Its language will therefore be more straightforward.

The theologian, on the other hand, is more likely to be making statements not only about faith but also about the teaching office's statements about faith. His concern is to look into the reasons that lead a particular statement about faith to be phrased in a particular way, with the object of discovering if the statement is an adequate expression of revealed truth. This will lead him to examine the extent to which a particular statement might have been historically conditioned and therefore perhaps now in part obsolete. Finally, he will try to develop a fresh formulation appropriate to the times.

2. It is in the nature of theology to make statements about doctrines that have no direct connection with the *depositum fidei*. Likewise, it will make judgments about arguments brought forward in support of particular doctrines. Critical examination of a statement is one of theology's functions and statements of the teaching office are not exempt. For this, freedom is clearly vital as without it the critical function could not be exercised, which in turn would mean theology's deflection from the search for truth. To pose questions about truth is an inalienable right of man, and also therefore of the theologian who is professionally equipped to exercise this right in the matter of Christian doctrine.

3. It is logically untenable for an institution to concede infallibility while at the same time claiming the right to settle questions of truth by virtue of its authority. Adequate argumentation alone can settle such issues. It would be desirable that in such cases the *magisterium* confined itself to a dialogue with the theologians, refuting their statements, where necessary, by counter-argument.

I am aware of being unable to contribute anything conclusive on this theme. But I shall be happy enough if what I have written were to lead to a discussion that was of service to the Church in these difficult times.

Translated by Simon King

Jean-Pierre Jossua

Rule of Faith and Orthodoxy

THE problem posed by "orthodoxy" at the present day is such that the mere mention of this term will provoke an attack against anyone imprudent enough to use it. It is as if merely raising the question of the orthodoxy of an expression of faith was as unacceptable to some as calling in question orthodoxy as an adequate concept for the determination of authentic faith is to others. Thus the term might be regarded as an especially sensitive indicator of the tense situation of faith itself in the Churches. In an attempt to explain the position and resolve the paradox I want to show that the question of the "rule of faith" is ineluctably raised at the very heart of faith—but that its interpretation as "orthodoxy", at least in practice, leaves out of account the historic character of Christianity, and therefore of faith itself, both in its realization and formulation.

I. Experience of Faith, Rule of Faith and Formulations of Faith

It is necessary to start with a hypothesis, failing which the discussion would have to be conducted differently: faith is not primary but it is the response to a saving act by God which, by the same token, is one of revelation. To avoid digression we can concentrate on one particular example which is at the same time the whole—Jesus Christ, the "Son of God"; we can consider christology and the Christian faith corresponding to it.

At the beginning, and as the basis of all Christianity, stands the *identification* of Jesus Christ. It is the paradox of a given transcendence, given up for salvation in an historical and human situation. It is the reconciliation of what is properly existential in man (the freedom of the Servant giving his life), of what is properly historical (the Master of the Beatitudes and of the *agape*, the prophet denouncing all unrighteousness and opening the modern history of mankind) with true transcendence: God *as* man, God *in* a situation of human freedom the maker of history.

Correspondingly, at the centre of all Christianity is a *determination* of faith—and of the whole of Christian existence—in strict relationship with christology, with the power of expressing itself as the paradox of an unconditional human adhesion to this commitment of God in Jesus Christ. That is, in its structure there is a duality of co-ordinated moments: it is radically new, different and cannot be mediated in history, and it can actually only be effected in earthly human life and in history. As the response to the challenge of the Other in Jesus Christ it comprises a time of radical difference, of absolute risk, gratuitousness and mysterious encounter which is symbolized in interpersonal categories; its particular act is prayer.

But as the encounter with the living God in his coming, in the world, in Jesus Christ, not only does it endow life on earth with meaning by acceptance of its plan, but it is only realized in action, in history—it knows its God only by commitment to his action of giving; its particular act is service.

In speaking of determination of faith, I meant not the form or content of its expression, but, more radically, the direction of its act as the correlative of the mystery of salvation itself. Actually, there can be no adequate separation of faith which believes (act) and faith which is believed (content). And as act it is not neutral in structure, or undetermined in direction—as though one could conclude that "a person believes" (no importance being attached to what he believes) and that, once a statement is held to be accurate a person believes (even if this belief comprises neither choice nor absolute risk).

To believe implies always interpreting what is believed; adherence alone, and finally the whole of existence, is interpretation. Especially, what is believed about Christ is given to us in all essentials in the actual determination of the act, a correlative of the determination of its "object".[1] What is believed is only the making explicit of both correlatives; the necessary transition to verbal expression—whether this be in scriptural symbols or in subsequent statements—is relative to the Mystery and to faith which is adjusted to it.

This is generally admitted, and my purpose is not to point out this relativity of statements, but to show that the question of the rule of faith goes beyond them and reaches the essential, the fundamental structure of faith which quite literally disappears when it is deformed. No distinction between the act of faith and its content is valid here; Christianity is based on a relationship determined right at its start; when this is lacking it becomes distorted and self-destructive.

There is therefore a standard, a rule of christology and faith, and this fundamental problem goes further than that of the correctness of the statements of it. Right faith is faith correctly determined in its orientation; it is then measured by the Mystery which it receives. But this must appear in the expression which it gives of this Mystery (symbols and statements).

What is this rule, and how is it to be applied in the reformulation of the truths of faith? The rule is that of the New Testament, itself the primary inspired and regulating expression of the faith of the community. But in view of the nature of the New Testament, the rule it supplies cannot be literally applied. The New Testament is a first and normative stage of interpretation and formulation—how could fresh interpretation and formulation be avoided? And how could it control this operation outside a living relationship with the conscience of the believer who can only restate his faith by reference to the recorded Word which as a whole both provokes it and gives it expression?[2]

I am convinced that the rule of faith cannot be conceived,

[1] I have put it thus for the sake of simplicity, for it is very important to recognize that the existential character of the manifestation of God in Christ enables us actually to resolve this dichotomy of objectivism and purely subjective actualism.

[2] Actually in the New Testament there are a number of symbolic expressions (christological titles, mysteries like the Cross, or the Ascension, whose symbolical content is considerable) or even statements whose definition as statements is contingent (anthropological structures): in both cases any form of simplistic fundamentalism is impossible.

whether it is a question of Scripture or ecclesiastical definitions, in terms of "orthodoxy"—and "heterodoxy", if by this is meant the "unchanging" (or even the "homogeneous")—and the "new". It seems to me that the history of Christian doctrine leads us to a conclusion which is only the expression of the historical nature of Christianity itself: any rule can only be proportional; it always refers therefore to something other than itself. It is essential to show this clearly.[3]

II. Formulations of Faith and History

1. We can begin with Christian doctrines in general and then go on to the specific case of "dogma". The true modern form of an unchanging orthodoxy is not complete fixity, whose case has been settled, but homogeneous development, the historicist transposition of fixity which "homogeneity" rescues from the dilemma to which the rejection of all history had brought it. But the uncritical idea of a progress is as apologetical as that of unchangeableness, and its optimistic form overlooks the main point of the historical phenomena of variation, which in principle it allows (substitution of one system of thought for another, regression, ideas fallen into oblivion, rediscoveries, and so on).

2. As a matter of fact the history of doctrines, in their relativity, shows clearly a series of *intelligible structures*. These represent the effort of a period, to the extent of its cultural resources, to systematize and grasp intellectually the whole body of symbols, experiences, convictions and behaviour patterns of Christian man. The *structure* is derived from the conjunction of *constituent elements* arising from a given cultural context, together with the *fundamental elements* of Christianity. The difficulty of the problem here is to discern the constant element in these latter without interpreting it as unchangeableness—for they are never to be seen as in a "chemically pure" state or isolated from any contingent formulation. In this way we can see the emergence of *partial*

[3] For this purpose I have summarized here the analysis developed at length in "Immutabilité, progrès, ou structurations multiples des doctrines chrétiennes", in *Revue Sc. Ph. Th.*, 52 (1968), pp. 173–200, which quotes various shades of meaning, important complementary ideas and frequent examples.

structures (the medieval doctrine of marriage, constructed on the Aristotelian system of the two ends). But this view can be widened to *general structures*: either *homogeneous systems* (Scotism), or, on the other hand, common guiding principles in a given cultural context but treated by it in different ways (theological science in the thirteenth century).

3. A first variability factor of these structures is obvious: the *variation in the constitutional elements* which affects the intelligible structure and in extreme cases diminishes its value. This is the modification through criticism or pragmatism of the climate common to the ambient philosophical theories and, more fundamentally, of the civilization whose reflection they are. New questions are raised, other views of things are discovered, spontaneous developments are criticized, and also certain aspects of reality are lost sight of.

In analysing this first factor, two modifying influences must be considered. The first is that the variation is never complete and that it will affect unequally the various fields concerned—cosmology, metaphysics, anthropology, and ethics. It is not a matter of regarding the variation of structures as a succession of totally discontinuous figures: they evolve, degenerate, and are renewed, until a new balance can be observed (which, superficially, might not look so different).

The second factor is that the rational structure or framework is modified at each period by Christianity: either these modifications are finally assimilated by their environment (a measure of Christian ethics in our civilization), or the guiding Christian hypothesis acts as the inspiration of philosophical reflection, forming a sub-culture (dependent on its setting, but not wholly "Christian philosophies").

Lastly, the second *variability* factor is the fluid nature of the *datum* which is itself *structured* according to the differences of emphasis and spiritual perception, the variously centred and harmonized intuitions which give rise to several "spiritualities" and also to the theological systems dependent on them: different schools at one and the same time, or the insights of a period, bound up with a given ecclesial context and with the more important experiences and doctrinal struggles of the time, and with the knowledge possessed of the Christian past.

4. The conjunction between the *structuring ambience* and the *structured element* leads therefore to a *structure*, an intelligible expression of the Christian experience of a given period. But this experience is itself caused, and then has light thrown upon it, by words from the past—in the first place by the Word. They form an intrinsic part of this experience and in it recover their meaning; but they are handed down to other times and possess a meaning for all times. Thus in the *structured element* there exists a state of tension between what is unchanging and its successive interpretations; this is a problem of hermeneutics which is a continuation of that of the interpretation of the Bible and of the interpretation in the Bible itself of previous traditions.

An interesting example of this tension is to be found in a certain number of leading ideas which stand out from the incomplete structures by reason of their relative stability after several re-readings. They remain more constant because they spring from a more original and enduring intention to give expression to certain logical aspects which are the consequences of faith. Of course, these leading ideas—christological theandrism, the anthropological paradox of man made for God and of himself incapable of attaining the end without which he cannot be himself—can never be expressed outside a particular cultural context. Or at least the same words undergo value changes according to context. But if the datum is never apprehended before being formulated, its recurrence is the sign of its existence and the comparison establishes its permanent nature. These leading ideas, of course, are derived from the *kerygma of the Church*, though they differ from it in their more abstract formulation. But the *kerygma* itself raises the same problems: its rediscovery occurs not through confrontation with a written Word, but in a living tradition, which implies that it be both understood and structured afresh.

The importance of this can be appreciated: theology is not purely and simply an analysis of the text in which the fundamental Word is recorded, nor is it interpretation with the aid merely of our present resources. The statement that it is the renewal of this Word in a tradition which enshrines all previous findings is not merely an assertion that the Word is recovered *in* this sequence, but that it is recovered *with* all its previous modes of expression.

5. In a given milieu, indeed, the form of the Christian message, in its essentials, could hardly have been different—even if room has been found for variations, for theological systems within a single general formulation. This very great intellectual effort in regard to the faith of past generations has something of crucial importance to offer us. The formulations which resulted from it, while establishing no norm, and simply because they were a successful solution to the problem of accounting for one aspect of faith, contain various lessons. Only one of these is mentioned here. If theological formulations are compared with reference to the datum and the leading ideas which they seek to explain, rules of structural stability are seen to emerge, the permanent but purely relative principles of theological science. These remain indispensable guides for subsequent reformulations. Devotion to the "Sacred Heart", and its theology in the seventeenth century, preserved an essential aspect of christology, and this effort, now buried in the past, is full of meaning for us, since it shows a determination to preserve a certain balance between God's divine majesty and his humanity.[4]

6. In the case of dogmas, our analysis must include the crucial variations which avoid relativism—but these formulations can scarcely be preserved on principle. Surely, the homogeneous development of dogma shows the same characteristics? (By "dogmas" are meant those doctrines which the judgment of the Church, connecting them with the Word as formal statements, consequences or explanations, but reformulating them in a given context, has stamped with her charism of indefectibility.)

A large number of doctrines which in other ages were regarded as dogmas are now no longer accepted as such. In other cases a difficult comparison has to be made between documents originating at different periods in the life of the Church (*Unam sanctam, Vehementer nos* and *Gaudium et spes*, for instance). My purpose here is more limited and hardly original. Everyone knows that in a dogma, an ecclesial formulation of the Word at a given period and place, a distinction must be made between its absolute authority deriving from the Word itself, and the authority of the

[4] There are many other examples in the article quoted in the previous note.

Church engaged upon its formulation. The latter, it is generally agreed, is dependent on time and place,[5] and this dependence gives rise to a legitimate diversity in dogmatic formulation itself.[6] On this view, it is not the term "homogeneous"—in contrast with actual evolution—which causes difficulty, but the term "development", in the singular; there are *developments*. Rational life in faith is productive, many-sided, and made up of approximations and investigations in various directions—and it is from this venturesome experience that dogmatic formulation originates.

7. When, on the basis of the events and words of salvation, the message is formulated in "professions of faith", it remains, none the less, more than a text: it is a living reality which is communicated, it is an inexhaustible experience which will continue to be deepened and to grow more explicit even when it is determined by Scripture. But new questions will arise and fresh possibilities of a better formulation of the message. It is in these circumstances that, in various contexts, Christian theological systems come into being and the proclamation of the message takes on different forms. How does the transition to "dogma" occur? Within a specific system of relationships it is possible, as we know, for there to be special constructions, partial realizations of the structure which, on account of cultural references and knowledge of the datum and tradition is common (christological theandrism, formulated in terms of the two natures—dyophysism). A particular formulation may appear as an inadequate attempt to express the fundamental datum and the traditional fundamental ideas (the christology of Eutyches, formulated in classical terms, and made dangerous by a new context). In this case theology or ecclesiastical authority can reject it or construct another formula making it normative (Chalcedon).

8. In the case of Scripture, "normative" means the privileged value given for all time to a symbolic expression or affirmation

[5] "For the deposit of faith or revealed truths are one thing; the manner in which they are formulated without violence to their meaning and significance is another."—Vatican II, *Gaudium et spes*, II, chapter 2, art. 62, repeating a speech by John XXIII (*AAS*, 54, 1962, p. 792).

[6] "The heritage handed down by the apostles was received in different forms and ways, so that from the beginnings of the Church it has had a varied development in various places, thanks to a similar variety of natural gifts and conditions of life." Vatican II, *Unitatis redintegratio*, III, art. 14.

of faith. Here, it means that given a certain context, some expression (two natures, one person) is a necessary transition to answer a certain question or to allow for a certain fundamental idea in this system of co-ordinates. Here again, then, there are two variability factors, one arising from the source (a different implication in the datum would change the problem), and the other from subsequent developments (another question, another context, would result in other formulations making the previous ones more remote). The new formulations do not make those preceding them wrong, since their fundamental purpose is safeguarded. It is so in the first place because once the problem is raised anew in the same terms as before, it remains necessary to formulate the answer *in this way*—the relative necessity to which appeal is made for the theological formulation is here given regular sanction (an aspect of ecclesial authority). Next, it is so because the *truth of faith* set out in this formulation must remain secure in any other context (an aspect of the authority of the Word in ecclesial formulation). Lastly, even the way in which a difficulty in formulating a definition was resolved, contains many lessons both for ordinary theological tradition and much else besides.

9. Anyone who at the present time wants to reformulate christology must keep the definition of Chalcedon firmly in mind, even if he does not adopt its categories or its wording. It remains an essential witness by reason of the preciseness of its terms and its balanced nature, even if, by its juxtaposition of the two natures, rectified by the communication of attributes, it does not match up to the full extent of our idea of the datum nor answer our most fundamental questions: for example, the insertion of God in history, the mystery of the humanity of Christ as humanity, Christ's personal knowledge. A more economical christology is not enough: God must be thought of *as* man, what this means for God, what this gives to man. Now what was said here at the beginning must show that this is so: if it is essential in christology, it is also for the whole concept of Christian life for its "worldliness" to be understood in proper proportion. A Christian life which is shown by and in a human life (and not on the level of the extraordinary or the marvellous) must be an integral life, comprising among its essential experiences a relation of sonship with God as a human activity. The necessity, indeed the difficulty, the

possible deviations of this twofold and unique operation will probably be lost on no one; in addition, the great value and the limitations of the contribution can be clearly seen.

10. Thus it is clear that the rule of faith is not an immutable formula, but a certain proportion of succeeding formulas bearing the mark of distinct contexts—and in the case of christology, a certain *balance*, which derives from the internal balance of the mystery of Christ and of the experience of faith to which it gives notional expression. It is clear, too, that such a rule could not be applied materially, but raises once again the question of the criterion.

III. Interpretation by the Community

What criterion can we discover to establish the rule of faith, discern aims and structure, confirm the fidelity of a re-interpretation and, in the formula and beyond it, establish the orientation of faith? If my analysis is correct, recourse to the textual records of the past will not provide this criterion, since such a recourse itself requires something else; it will be found in an appeal to that living consciousness which we have seen at work in the past to produce these texts. We have discovered a process extending from the infallibility of the Church to the norm or (proportional) infallibility of its documents. This path must be travelled in the opposite direction and, from the static, return to the dynamic criterion, the criterion in action which is the actual source of the other.

In the light of the Word and with the help of tradition a new assessment must be made of what is contingent in the past; its purpose must be elucidated to recover its theological implications or, on occasion, to assess other attempts. Of course, for the man anxiously seeking safety, there will be no certain foothold. It will be a matter of re-interpretation of the biblical symbols, returning to the events of salvation and Christian experience in tradition by a community—and it is its faith which will form the judgment. Once more the importance of this tradition of Scripture must be emphasized—not as the mere material transmission of an immutable tradition, nor as an illusory and continual embellishment or coming to maturity, nor indeed as a mere cultural continuity effecting contemporaneity in every age; rather is it a living medium in which the Spirit bestows a connaturality with Scripture, indefectibly transmitting the Word and with it the accumulated store of an age-long meditation, now offered for our investigation.

I mentioned *community* to avoid involvement in difficult distinctions which are outside the scope of this article. In addition, it would be necessary to include also the aspect of ecclesial authority in relation to the unanimous proclamation of the Word and to the verification of its connection with the origins. Catholic ecclesiology allows us to affirm this charism existing in the Church; it distinguishes and gives expression to the unfailing action of the Spirit in the community. As regards "orthodoxy",[7] the problem is not to deny or minimize hierarchical interventions, without at the same time being involved in the problem of membership or non-membership, which would be bound up with juridical criteria arbitrarily settled by authority. There can be no question of relying on authority so that it becomes the criterion, nor of accepting as equivalent "living tradition" and *"magisterium"*.

There is a still further important consequence which will shed some light on the position which formed our starting-point. When it is a matter of interpretation several of them are possible. There is room for a certain pluralism in the community; some sort of research leading to a relative diversity is indispensable. But it is no small problem to touch a completely fixed system such as Catholicism wished, or thought itself, to be, since in actual fact it did not cease to evolve. It is no small matter when a whole body without fault or division, one that is absolute and endowed with an intense affective attachment, is shown to be far more composite, frail and relative. In that case, how can it be avoided that what is essential is no longer clearly seen, and that even the return to the essential, which is always a matter of interpretation, is carried out in the wrong way?

Actually, in addition to necessary forms of pluralism, there can be forms of renewal which in the process of interpretation change

[7] It is obvious that the term "orthodoxy" is patient of a meaning different from the orthodoxy (=immutability) criticized here, and that it can be equated with what we term "rule of faith".

the identification of Christ and the determination of faith. We know that these interpretations are in existence at the present time; by their rejection of any rule of faith, they raise for the community the question of fundamental fidelity to its origin. Take, for example, the christology of "Christianity without God" (Jesus, the master of brotherly love and an example of risk), that of the "theologians of the death of God" (kenosis without Subject or resurrection), that of strict Bultmannism (outstanding for the vigour of its faith, but Docetist through its narrow existential criterion applied to our existence alone and not to our Saviour's humanity); then there is the christology of Bishop John Robinson of *Honest to God* (man for the sake of others, revealing by the depth of his love for the mystery of God, but telescoping Christ's filial dialogue with his Father); lastly, and more serious still, perhaps, though still in an irreproachably orthodox way, there is the example of the Docetism of the integrists for whom the human—and on a last analysis, the political—significance of the life of Christ are emptied of meaning. These christologies, precisely in their disproportionate nature, are correlatives of the many mutilations or contradictions in the concept of Christian life which now abound.

In my view the community will finally be obliged to make a choice, for the straining of language has become too great. It brings into being real latent schisms—without a break occurring, since interpretation allows this diversity which immutability (even imagined) excluded. This choice, often made in the past by Churches under the influence of the Spirit, will have to be made afresh. The rule of faith remains indispensable: it is of great importance that it should be applied neither too soon—in a simplistic way—nor too late.

Translated by Lancelot Sheppard

Bernard-Dominique Dupuy

The Constitutive Nature of Ethics in the Confession of the Christian Faith

THE emphasis of Christian thought in recent centuries has been on the distinction between theology and morals; that they are complementary to each other has been far less clearly affirmed. In consequence a certain hiatus, a cleavage, sometimes even an actual opposition, has appeared between theology in the strict sense, the field of the intellect, and ethics, the field of action, of *praxis*. In our own time, on the contrary, Christians stress the ethical aspect of the gospel. They assert that the Christian message has moral, social and even political dimensions. This assertion implies that it is possible to proceed logically from the traditionally confessed faith and from the morality of Christianity to those questions which arise in moral and social life, in economic and political reality. It acknowledges that if, in the world in which we live, there is a certain discordance between daily action and culture, between life and language, the faith cannot ignore it. It sees that the crisis of modern man leads to searching questions, from which the Christian conscience cannot feel itself estranged. It implies that the realities of faith, of tradition, of the Christian life, are in some way refracted in day-to-day existence, which is lived under new forms, unknown to the ancient world, and can be rediscovered there.

I. Difficulties in Thinking about Christian Ethics

To affirm, in our day, the ethical dimensions of Christianity means not only to postulate the connection between morals and dogma as self-evident, but also to make an act of faith; it means to demonstrate that there must be a link between the traditional Christian ethic, which is in the line of contemplation, wisdom and "virtue", and contemporary secular ethics, in the line of accomplished fact, of lived reality, of *praxis*. We shall be justified in this claim and this attempt if we show precisely that the Judaeo-Christian revelation does not admit the separation of the two planes, the dogmatic and the ethical, that it rejects the idea of their opposition and is not responsible for the cleavage which has grown up between them over the ages.

It is not my intention here to invoke a Christian ethic which should be independent of the problems of the present world, to be taken in itself. Such a concept is even less conceivable for ethics than for dogma. An ethic is lived in the concrete. One must examine it from the starting-point of the world in which men live, taking account of its wants, its insufficiencies, its defects, and see how it is precisely its wants which can illuminate the situation which the Judaeo-Christian revelation comes to illuminate. It is the world as it is which demands an ethic and waits for the message of revelation. It is at this point of contact between the world and the Church that the problem of the Christian ethic must be faced.

1. An initial difficulty in any general reflection on the ethics of Christianity stems from the vast scope of the field of ethics. All human life is embraced. That is why certain exegetes have advanced the thesis that Jesus never gave his disciples any system of ethics, that the gospel in certain texts simply presents the current ethics of the first century, until the time when the Christian ethic, whose foundations were laid by Paul, could be formulated. Thus there would have been an "interim ethic", which is easily understood when we consider that the first Christians were expecting the coming of the *Parousia* and had no idea of organizing the world. But what has happened, in our days, to the formation of the Christian ethic? Has it followed the same rhythm as the formation of dogma?

2. A second difficulty: it must be stressed that the Western world, which is sometimes said to represent Christian civilization, often systematically disregards its Judaeo-Christian origins. Yet its sources are well known. Rational in its action, sometimes spiritual,

sometimes materialist in outlook, the West draws on its Greek and Latin sources, but is strikingly ignorant of its biblical source. Some Christians, of course, helped by the contemporary discovery of salvation-history, are beginning to examine themselves by the ethics of the prophets and the message of the apostles. But, a few promising signs apart, the Western Christian world is only slowly recovering the key to a behaviour based on revelation. The Greek tradition, on the whole, tends to contrast the pure contemplation of ideas, regarded as unchangeable realities, with the flux of heraclitean becoming, the discontinuities of concrete action. No doubt Plato felt acutely the discordance between the unchangeable realities and daily life, and he saw more clearly than anyone else the need at all costs to unite them: he made philosophy go down into the cave. But that was the intuition of a great thinker, and on the whole the Greek tradition opposes contemplation to action. This, at least, is the conclusion of Pierre-Maxime Schuhl:[1] Greek civilization is built up on the contrast between the liberal and the mechanical arts; it lives on the intuition of two dissociated worlds.

This dissociation is found again in the Latin world, and it has left its mark on the Christian tradition. We all know the usual interpretation of the story of Martha and Mary: Jesus says of Mary's *faith*: "She has chosen the better part, which shall not be taken away from her." The conclusion has been drawn, in the Greek sense, that the *contemplative life* is above the *active life*, is of a higher value in itself, and this has led to distinguishing two modes of practising the Christian life: the contemplative and the active. The great Christian mystics, of course, St Francis of Assisi, St Teresa of Avila, St Vincent de Paul, rose above the contrast, but the ability to do so has tended to remain the privilege of the saints than become part of the institution. Generally speaking, the problem of action and the spiritual life has not been resolved in a genuine unity.

These ideological and spiritual perspectives are found on the level of the social structures. In the article quoted above, P. M. Schuhl observes that, according to the biblical view of man, every man must follow Adam by earning his bread through the sweat

[1] Pierre-Maxime Schuhl, "Lecture et contemplation", in *Efforts et réalisation* (Dec. 1952).

of his brow, not leaving this care to a particular social class, which is what tends to happen in society. Ancient slavery and medieval serfdom both tend to distribute the incidence of the primeval curse: some bear it directly, while others have the leisure to escape into the life of the spirit. The tasks are divided among specialized "orders", which are the foundation of social life, and these traditions are psychologically and objectively defended, because they seem perfectly natural.

II. Revelation as Knowledge and as Encounter

In these conditions, how can the meaning of man implicit in the Bible gain a hearing? How can the ethics proper to salvation-history be realized in a world where social relations are in no respect based on revealed ethics? How, in short, can the message of the Bible reach and affect the world?

The usual answer is: by the *kerygma* and the preaching of the faith, then by acknowledging the Church and submitting to the *magisterium*. Very true; but this schema presents, to use Maurice Blondel's terminology, an extrinsical character, and corresponds hardly at all to reality.

The Bible teaches us, in fact, that everything begins with an *event*, unexpected and decisive, a fresh start. Abraham leaves Ur; the Hebrews, united by Moses, escape from the hand of Pharaoh. That event is always something in the thick of history, it is not something in the realm of ideas. The God of the philosophers is a concept derived from abstract ideas; the God encountered by the patriarchs and prophets is revealed in events and actions. Entry into a new life, then, is not primarily adherence to a moral code or a body of doctrine, but faithfulness to the saving events. Believing means that memory, it means entering into the permanent presence of a sacred event. It is not only accepting a truth of dogmatic character, or following a code of morals. Loyalty to the faith is expressed in the celebration of the events of salvation, in which the recitation of the creed is included, but it is not reduced to the recitation of the creed. To ignore the event, when entering into the event is precisely what matters, and to be concerned only with the teaching which may have been drawn from it is to lose an essential aspect of Christianity.

This event comes to us as an *encounter*, a meeting. If the term "event" has a rather neutral character, the term "encounter" leads us to the very heart of ethics. Every encounter is in truth a meeting with another, with a "thou" (to employ the categories of Martin Buber), and, through that "thou", an invocation of the "eternal Thou". If we had to interpret this encounter with the eternal Thou in the classical Thomist categories, we could say that it corresponds to the recognition of the *veritas prima* (*in cognoscendo*) which is accomplished in the act of faith. We know, in fact, that the act of faith *non terminatur ad enunciabile, sed ad rem*. The transcendent God touches the mind as a subject, and the mind meets God in the manner of an object. The believer comes face to face with the Other, darkly glimpsed.

In the categories of modern thought, in which understanding is characterized not so much by the hold of an object on the mind as by the subjective activity of the reason, the meeting with the eternal Thou is seen not as a "knowing" but rather as what Martin Buber calls an "actualization" (*Verwirklichung*).[2]

This "actualization" which presides over the act of faith upsets our categories of thought, all founded, since Descartes and even more since Kant, on the theory of knowledge based on the subject-object relationship. To a Buber, the case of God (if one can call it so), the case of revelation, is the one which can least, if at all, be expressed in terms of subject and object. We must therefore appeal to other categories than those of the understanding. God is *encountered*, he is never *known* in the capacity of an object. The register of "actualization" necessarily withdraws us from that of objectivation and speculation. Martin Buber refuses to study revelation from the angle of theology if the only result of that study is to reinstate in the domain of faith a knowledge which would be a partial human grasp of God, that is, if it simply made revelation an object of our speculation.

Now revelation is not an object for speculation, but it is the source of "actualization". It does not reveal God's being to us; it inaugurates human life according to God. "Revelation does not concern the mystery of God, it concerns the life of man, if by that

[2] Martin Buber, *Daniel. Gespräche von der Verwirklichung* (Leipzig, 1913); English translation *Daniel* (London and New York, 1964). *Ich und Du* (Leipzig, 1923); English translation, *I and Thou* (Edinburgh, 1960).

we mean a life which can and must be lived in function of the mystery of God; or more accurately, a life which is truly lived thus, if there is to be an authentic life." Another Jewish thinker, Abraham Heschel, puts it in similar terms: "The Bible is not a theology for man; it is an anthropology for God."[3]

In this register of reflection on revelation, the way by which to recognize the action of God in the world is not so much what we call theology as anthropology and ethics, for revelation appears on the path of the existent in an *ethos* far more than by the *logos*. This fact has already been underlined by Newman in his *Idea of a University*

This register of human behaviour brings into play quite another set of qualities besides pure intellect. The attitude of benevolent neutrality and static openness, typical of the intellectual act, must here give place to one of interior tension, of active communication, which sets in motion spiritual and creative energies. Through the encounter, these energies are roused in the heart of a reciprocity of *consciences* and not only as acts of our *faculties*. Here, under quite new categories, we touch on the very idea of revelation. In the encounter, it is existence itself which is revealed, it is being which is manifested. There is revelation of being, because existence then becomes word, is revealed in what Buber calls the "verbal" character of being. He who faces me, perceived and welcomed, does not remain dumb; he speaks, and his word, offered to my appeal, calls forth the response of my being. Revelation creates the world of dialogue.

The man who seeks to "know" is *interested* in an object. It is different with the man who "actualizes"; he is *concerned* by the event which happens to him, by the encounter to which he is called. The object apprehended, if it interests me, leaves me master of myself, while it allows me, in a certain capacity, to become its master. On the contrary, the Other, encountered as a Thou, affects me, alters my trajectory and my destiny, changes me. The knowledge of an object introduces to my mind a likeness of that object, which I can *evoke* whenever I like. "Actualization" does more, it invests the one who stands before me with the

[3] Abraham Heschel, *Les bâtisseurs du temps* (Paris, 1954). *Dieu en quête de l'homme. Philosophie du judaïsme* (Paris, 1968), p. 434; English translation *Between God and Man* (London, 1965).

dignity and uniqueness of the Other, of the Thou whom I *invoke*, of the face which shows itself, the personality which unveils itself and enters, suddenly, into my existence. Knowledge is appropriation. "Actualization" opens the door to the encounter with another, and is disappropriation.

III. Tradition: Education rather than Instruction

If revelation is essentially encounter rather than knowledge in the intellectualist sense of the word, tradition is education rather than instruction. The object of religious education is to establish the relationship between man and God, and expresses the holiness of God, in a sense which is worlds away from the possession or capture of something sacred or numinous, such as we find in the primitive religions, or in the mystery religions. In those religions, the possession of God by man, or of man by God, through the mediation of a mystagogue, in "enthusiasm" or ecstasy, is presented as the consequence of the encounter with God, the beginning of the spiritual life. Judaism and genuine Christianity have always been hostile to these forms of secret instruction; they denounce them as idolatry. The numinous exalts man's faculties or else transports them beyond their natural capacities. True freedom, restored by the Judaeo-Christian revelation, is opposed to these "transports". The numinous destroys the relationship between persons by trying to project them, through ecstasy, into a *drama* where beings are lost. This esoteric idea is the opposite of the sacrament, which is *memorial*, the entry into an event which concerns me and makes me invoke the living God.

Judaeo-Christian monotheism does not exalt any sacred power, does not feed on multiple miracles, for it plunges into the heart of human existence. There is a rabbinical midrash which well expresses this sense that human existence is at the heart of revelation. It represents God as teaching both angels and Israel. In this school of divine education, the angels ask Israel, seated in the front ranks, to explain the divine word to them. This parable teaches us that human life, despite its inferior rank, is the true place where the divine word makes itself understood, where it becomes intelligence. But the object of the parable is also to make us understand that the truth of the angels is not of another kind from the truth of men, and that men attain to the revelation without any ecstasy coming to tear them from their nature, from their human existence.

Tradition thus understood, as education in the true religious relationship and as entry into the path traced by salvation history, is the key to the Christian mystery in totality and as totality, beyond all that can be understood or formulated about it. Beyond, too, anything that can be justified by external references, historical or critical. It is verified by the fact that it is not the work of any isolated individual, but of a whole people. the Church. It thus constitutes, in its totality and coherence, an autonomous principle of discernment.

This character of tradition has been particularly developed by Maurice Blondel in *Histoire et dogme*.[4] In the thick of the debate provoked by the modernist exegesis, Blondel showed that the Christian faith, while dependent on historico-critical evidences external to Scripture and tradition, is not adequately measured by them. Tradition draws from a source which is permanent, incorruptible, never to be reduced to written documents or a private interpretation: the *experience of reality* formed by the life of the whole believing community, united around the successors of the apostles. That experience is not the work of some individuals, but of an entire people, the Church, and it constitutes thenceforth an original principle of continuity and discernment of the truth. Blondel demonstrated the originality of tradition, thus envisaged, in relation to all teaching and to every form of doctrinal *magisterium*: it is the progressive and permanent grasp of the treasure possessed by the Church as a reality of life. It is, since the beginning of Christianity, a sort of kept promise and a given possibility of action, in the heart of the Christian community.

> Tradition brings to distinct awareness elements hitherto concealed in the depths of faith and practice, rather than expressed, stated or reflected on. So this conserving and preserving power helps both to instruct and to initiate. Looking lovingly to the past, where its treasure is, it advances towards the future, where lies its victory and its light. Even when it discovers something, it feels humbly that it is

[4] Article in *La Quinzaine* (Jan.–Feb. 1904), reproduced in *Les premiers écrits de Maurice Blondel* (Paris, 1956), pp. 149–228.

faithfully recovering it. It has nothing to innovate, for it possesses its God and its all; but it always has something new to teach us, for it brings something on from the implicitly lived to the explicitly known. Whoever, in short, lives and thinks christianly is working for it; the saint who perpetuates Jesus among us, as well as the scholar who goes back to the pure sources of revelation, or the philosopher who strives to open the ways of the future and to prepare the perpetual birth of the Spirit of newness. And this diffused work of the members contributes to the health of the body, under the guidance of the head, who alone, in the unity of a divinely assisted consciousness, unifies and stimulates its progress.

Blondel recognized in tradition a faculty of keeping and holding the totality of the deposit of faith, which conscious and reflected thought does not guarantee to the same degree. "Action has this privilege, that it is clear and complete, even in the implicit, whereas thought, with its analytical character, takes the form of knowledge only by a slow and groping reflection. And that is why it seems to me essential to combine dogmatic knowledge, always perfectible, with the Christian life, which does not need explicit knowledge to be perfect." These explanations of Blondel's do not involve any concession to pragmatism. They are the expression of a datum of faith, equally recognized by Newman. The faithful, who do not possess an explicit knowledge nor a complete instruction about tradition, none the less carry on that living tradition and guard it with certainty in the most acute moments of crisis.[5] The Christian life has a priority over theological research and rash ideological expressions. Faith is transmitted in life, in a lived practice, far more than in words. One must believe and live as men have lived before us, since the apostles, since Christ, in the heart of the community of the brethren. Whoever innovates in that respect puts himself outside the Catholic tradition.

This transmission of the faith in a community *praxis* has its higher levels. It is expressed in the *rites*. Here we should give the

[5] Cf. J. H. Newman, *On Consulting the Faithful in Matters of Doctrine*, appeared as an article in *The Rambler* (July, 1859); see also edition edited by J. Coulson (London, 1961). Cf. J. Lebreton, "Le désaccord de la foi populaire et de la théologie savante dans l'Eglise chrétienne au IIIe siècle", in *Revue d'Histoire ecclésiastique*, 19 (1923), pp. 481–506, and 20 (1924), pp. 5–37.

notion of rite its broadest possible sense, and use it if possible in the singular, for the rite embraces not only the liturgical action and the forms of prayer but also the customs, the rules of law, the cultural and spiritual habits of the community. It is a style of life, a manner of being a Christian in the world, and a means by which Christians recognize one another. Concretely speaking, there is room for a plurality of rites in the Christian regime, because of the possible diversifications in the Christian community. But this diversity of rites does not affect the essential structure of the rite in its essential moments: baptism and the Eucharist. The sacrament is thus the essential place of tradition. We could say that it is its "theological place". There the faith is transmitted in its totality, at once instruction, principle of life and salvation, catechesis and sacrament, "mystery" in the sense of the saving act of Jesus Christ, operating now in the sacred signs apprehended by faith. Gregory of Nyssa called baptism the *proté paradosis*, the first tradition, and baptism in its beginnings ascribed the fullest importance to the *traditio* (and a few days later the *redditio*) *symboli*. Baptism was the entry into a community whose way of life one was assimilating, and whose rules of conduct one observed. By the sacraments one entered into the living reality of Christianity.

IV. The "Sensus Fidei" as Ethical Sense and Style of Life

The effect of tradition on the faithful is to communicate to them what the Fathers and the councils called the *Catholic sense* or the *sense of the faith*. This sense of the faith is the living profession of faith of all the faithful, in its continuity and age-long identity. It is not a theoretical profession of faith, couched in formulas; it is rather the way of being a Christian today, following those who were Christians yesterday and preparing those who will be so tomorrow. It is an act of the Catholic community. Thus understood, the *sensus fidei* cannot be reduced to the profession of faith; it is the very stuff of Christianity. *Non terminatur ad enunciabile*.... It is the effect of the baptismal initiation. It has been offered up in the *redditio symboli*; it is a certain instinct of what is required of me in order that I may live in the communion of the Church, and that the communion of the Church may be developed through me. That is why it has sometimes been called *sensus catholicus*, not in the sense that the believer ought to adhere to every doctrinal proposition to be met in the Catholic tradition, but in the sense that the believer lives in communion with the whole Catholic body. The Christian sense, put into practice by the faithful in their life and action, is thus a maker of communion. It is a maker of unity and truth and contributes to the Church's indefectibility.

Translated by Patrick Hepburne-Scott

Michel de Certeau

Is there a Language of Unity?

Broken Unity: Some Preliminary Considerations

PLURALISM, before becoming at Vatican II[1] a doctrine or a programme, was a fact. But it is now undergoing development beyond the limits allowed by the most "liberal" theories. It is assuming the appearance of an insuperable division. Unity, made flexible by the admission of variations, is being lost in this multiplicity. Where among so many opposing views is it to be seen? By what signs is it to be discerned among so many divergent experiments which all claim the same name and call themselves Christian, whether it be a question of the same faith, the same Lord or the same baptism?[2] Christianity is breaking up into pieces each claiming the title of genuine, but the label attaching to each could well be no more than a fiction, and an equivocal sign between differently named convictions, communities or concepts. Though the Church professes diversity and the authorities admit the principle (but not always its consequences), the effective decomposition is far more advanced than the official statements seem inclined to admit; it appears dangerous because it threatens unity and even makes the possibility of it doubtful.

Thus a movement in the opposite direction occurs. The admission (of diversity) is toned down, because it is now considered to be excessive and rash, as if it were the cause of the "evil" or as if it had aggravated it, whereas it was only an additional symptom

[1] Especially in the texts about ecumenism and mission.
[2] Ephes. 4. 4–6.

and the prudent manifestation of an actual situation. Even if the stated principles are left untouched there is some temptation to modify or restrict their application, to slow down the "democratization" of institutions and by means of the system of representation imposed on the various movements in the Church, to prevent their effective manifestation. Then, too, there is the attempt to oblige Christians who "differ" to return to a reaffirmed tradition or cut themselves off from the Church by giving up their own witness to Jesus Christ. In short, the temptation is to restrict the great amount of research and endeavour and to detach from this ebullient and uncontrollable profusion of experience a section considered "conformist" and *orthodox*.

Necessary Unity

Such a reaction is becoming frequent. It is evidence of a certain anxiety and from that stage it can easily become defensive, apologetic and even accusatory. But it cannot be explained away by fear, nor can it be reduced to the level of the denunciations that it sometimes provokes. It has a meaning. It reminds us of a *necessity* of faith, that is, the possibility of giving social expression, through recognizable signs, to the unity of God which is manifested in the plurality of Christian experiences. It would become impossible to believe in the one God revealed in Jesus Christ if the witnesses testifying to him did not possess "something" in common. No one could call himself Christian if this term only had meanings which were unrelated to one another. All Christianity would be an illusion if it were unsuccessful in showing forth effective continuity and unity. It would only be a story, a fantasy of the night, a utopian and imaginary "faith" with no roots in history if it did not possess its own language and did not succeed in manifesting its spiritual coherence clearly.

Even when defensive in form (it is not always so) the reaction provoked at the present time by the "break-up" of the Church is therefore an expression of a fundamental requirement of faith.

It would be unrealistic only to dwell on its polemical aspects. But this "reaction", being too dependent on the internal divisions and controversies in the Church, is often content to give expression to a necessity without at the same time satisfying it. When it sets out to restore the (theological or liturgical) landmarks of faith, but only by identifying them with those of a present-day group, or of a development in the past, it increases the problem to which it draws attention. It shows the urgency of the matter but it does nothing to deal with it. It confines itself to showing clearly the division between the multiplicity of Christian experiences and the need of a dogmatic *locus* in which they can be recognized. The very steps intended to get rid of the gap in fact widen it; they lead to a reciprocal hardening of positions of opposing "truths".

Because we are here dealing with vital questions, and in the last analysis with truth, we are all affected by reasoning of this kind. By reducing truth to what we believe and experience, by defending what has become essential for us, we cut ourselves off from each other and are in danger of losing sight of the meaning of *Christian*, the very meaning to which we appeal by calling ourselves followers of Jesus Christ.

We must return ("return" is the biblical word for conversion) to the characteristics of the "Catholic" faith in Jesus Christ. This is a necessary preliminary to the twofold analysis to be elaborated here:

1. The data of the problem at present facing the Church must be stated freely. This submissive freedom in the face of the facts implies that God is "greater" than we are. There is no reason to fear for him. We know that reality is the sole way of approach to his truth. By hiding from ourselves the nature and effective forms of the present divisions, we should condemn ourselves to seeking God only in illusion or to ceasing to believe him a *reality*.

2. An attempt must be made to *respond here and now to the one God*, to determine the ways and conditions which will enable the unity which is fundamental to our faith to be signified socially and visibly, that is, really.

Truth: A Question of Conscience

Judging by the form in which it is lived, Christian experience has always manifested two inseparable though apparently contradictory aspects. All of us feel the effect of these two requirements, even if both are not felt equally.

The first is rooted rather more particularly perhaps in a long-standing philosophical tradition. It always prevails whenever it is a question of "truth" and wherever conscience asserts its authority. It is an absolute surpassing any other allegiance, even that of friendship or affection: *Magis amicus veritati.* There is a fundamental quality about it giving it priority which cannot be betrayed without betraying oneself and which, endowing life with a meaning, ultimately is more valuable than life. It is "something" ineradicable (yet perishable, for any compromise effaces it and gradually deflects it) which must be pursued and stated clearly. It is a truth without which living would no longer have a meaning. Weak and sometimes flickering like the coastal lights at night seen from a ship, this continually awaited light passes judgment on each statement and line of conduct. It is the mainspring inherent in and inspiring a language of words and gestures. It forms both its progress and its meaning. Inseparably bound up with each expression it is its whole reason for existence.

Christian language, because it claims to proclaim the Truth, is necessarily related to this requirement of conscience. It is no longer conceivable as being true if it does not correspond to this "absolute", if it does not give rise to it or ceases to represent for each believer the way of stating the indispensable truth without which life is not possible. It is legitimate only if it admits of this truthfulness of conscience and if, both controlled by it and revealing what it is, it enables it to be expressed in words and actions. In other words (as the gospel has already shown) Christian language is conditioned (as it is also "proved") by its power to be recognized as a necessity, whether personal or collective, prompting the remark, "It is true", or "How true it is!" Its value is to be measured by the fact that it is *received in the name of a requirement of conscience* and that it reveals it. Among very many others Marie de l'Incarnation wrote, "Everything came from the very centre of my soul."[3]

Through this first aspect Christian language ultimately implies that God is the truth of man. Man's essential relationship with God, as stated by the language of faith, is therefore the criterion of each language; it forms its ultimate "content", its final meaning and root. And so it is not in fact *possible* for Christian language in any form to downgrade the affirmation by conscience of

[3] Marie de l'Incarnation, *Œuvres*, 2 (ed. Jamet) (Desclée de Brouwer, Bruges and Paris, 1930), p. 427.

its present relationship with God and with God's love . . . poured into our hearts through the Holy Spirit who has been given to us",[4] in order to compel recognition on behalf of a past or a society. If Christian language were exempted from this form of control, it would amount to the elimination of the very truth given to the believer in the pain and desire of his own existence.

It follows that experiences of the absolute condition the truth of the language. The experience of faith is what the official language of faith must state and accept—what it affirms and what it judges. Hence the importance and the gravity of the relationship between Christian "experiences" (which also are languages of faith) and the doctrinal or dogmatic formulations: if this necessary link is relaxed, if it becomes questionable, if it is severed, of what "Christian" *truth* can doctrinal teaching still speak?

A Shared Truth: The Community

Christian language nevertheless fills another requirement, equally necessary to faith and showing that the truth is not to be identified with the knowledge of it that is possessed. To put it in its simplest form this imperative experienced by every believer can be stated as follows: "You, who are *another*, are necessary to my truth."

This experience is related to faith and charity: to faith which discovers God as more "other" and more "necessary"; to theological charity which is continually learning to respect the difference in others and to seek them as inseparable. It is the same movement here inspiring faith in God and love of the neighbour. From the point of view of truth (as it is experienced by the Christian in very different ways, whether developed or not) this necessary relation with the Other as with others is probably something specifically Christian. In any case it adds to the personal or collective absolute experience of these two elements: there are other truths than mine: I cannot be separated from them without ceasing to be in the way of truth. Each individual in turn discovers this insuperable differentiation and this necessary union. According to the period of history, and also the time of life, one or other of these two aspects is felt more strongly, but they correspond

[4] Rom. 5. 5.

with each other, they lead from one to the other, by their conjunction they characterize the whole of Christian experience. The difference, which can never be eliminated, arouses the desire for unity, and unity, being never achieved, re-establishes the difference. A constant "effort" makes God "nearer" to us or "stranger", and our brothers more "remote" or "closer".[5]

The community is the living sign of this experience: it can never be reduced to identity (by elimination of differences, the domination of a small number, the formalism of rules or projects, and so on). Nor is it compatible with pure dispersal (by mutual exclusion, by rejection of the truth to which others bear witness, by each individual wrapped up in his own private world). And so, what is *language* if it is not in actual fact the manifestation of the community, the statement of the experience that it implies? Continually language admits the differences and transforms them into the constituent of communication. It discloses opposing views but does so by virtue of those experiences which are mutually necessary for God's revelation to the individual.

Following the viewpoint which emphasizes the "question of conscience", the Christian will inquire: "What does a language matter to me if it is *not true for me*?" He is right but he must also add on behalf of a faith that cannot be dissociated from the Christian community: "What does a faith matter to me if it separates me from my brothers?"

These are not, however, two contradictory formulas. Rather, they combine together so as to constitute, renew and continue a language which is never "closed"—nor reserved to the museum of the past, to the dominance of the present or the confines of a special place. The first formula reminds us that God is the *truth of man* and that he cannot be held to be "the" truth if he is not at the same time "my" truth. The second means that God is God, that he is no one's property although he is present in each existence: the reality of his coming *and* of his remoteness is actually shown by the language of community, that is by the *union* of different witnesses, by the *magisterium* which represents and makes present the foundation of this union. It is shown too by

[5] Cf. Michel de Certeau, "Apologie de la différence", in *Études* (Jan. 1968), pp. 81–106; "L'Étranger", in *Études* (Mar. 1969), pp. 401–8, etc.

the need for the individual to acknowledge other experiences without rejecting his own, by a mutual respect founded on the relation of each believer with God, and by a reciprocal process never completed which, far from denying the truth of each profession of faith, presupposes it but refers back to other, different ones which are also necessary.

Two Temptations: Social Unity and Spiritual Exile

Seen in this way, the interplay of those two Christian requirements defines the language of faith. It must be accepted or stated by each individual as the expression of an "absolute" experience. In the name of a truth transcending all individual experience it must also allow exchange, circulation, confrontation and recognition between the affirmations of faith that are usually dissimilar at different times and in different places. In this way it manifests a relationship in the same Spirit between various functions in the Church.[6] Its acceptance is subject to the control of individual experience; to ensure its propagation in the community it must withstand the individuality of each believer. It is judged by experience of which it is also itself the judge.

Actually, the process of development of the language of faith gives rise to tensions (evident from the beginning and throughout Christian history). It is different, also, according to the manner of its representation in each group and society: the congregation (liturgy), teaching (catechesis, pastoral methods, and so on). From this arise the confrontations and comparisons which concern not merely "tendencies" connected with places and periods, but also functions which are necessarily distinct, "charisms" to preserve, and tasks which are irreconcilable with each other.

From this conspectus of normal conflicts must be separated two temptations which any important crisis renders more acute. At a time of change, when cultural, social and political differences become more pronounced, when, as at the present time, there is a great difference between the "many voices of our age"[7] and therefore also between the forms of Christian experience, the believer experiences more difficulty in tolerating these differences and in grasping their significance. He is therefore apt to choose, to the

[6] Cf. 1 Cor. 12. 4–11.
[7] *Gaudium et Spes*, 44, 1–3.

detriment of the other, one of the two aspects of Christian truth that have been differentiated above. It is a choice not without danger for by neglecting one side of a scheme necessary to Christian language he deprives the other of the very factor which makes it a "symbol" of the faith.

The first reaction consists in giving a privileged place to union, to defending the customary institutions and formulations, in believing them to be objectively true without taking into account new experiences and the difficulties encountered by many Christians in still accepting signs which had hitherto found such acceptance. For that reason this language no longer bears witness to the authenticity of experience. It bears no relation to the Spirit received by each believer and is cut off from this essential form of control. Without its being realized, perhaps, it is made independent of *truth* in order to sustain the community. It is consequently governed by the law of social utility; it forms the means of strengthening the group (even if the members of the group no longer hold, personally, all the truths that are stated). It is meant to safeguard the society of believers more than the truth of God who speaks through it.

In this way an objective factor is established which becomes both the rallying point and the guiding line of the community. It is connected less with the experience of Christians than with the needs of their organization; it is imposed rather than accepted and tends to contradict what it should communicate. As a matter of fact, while on the one hand the gift of God and his spiritual presence is affirmed, recourse to the various forms of witness to this presence is minimized for reasons of public utility. Questioning or verification of official declarations is made to appear questionable whereas fundamentally it amounts to the necessary verification by the Christian people of the degree to which they accept this teaching and acknowledge it as their own truth. In extreme cases, to preserve the unity of the body, the stage is reached at which its Spirit is feared, and it is even believed that God has lived but that he no longer bears witness to himself and no longer lives on today in the recipients of his messages.

Excuses are made for this way of subjecting expressions of the Truth to the interests of a group, for using them to support an authority or preserve some form of autonomy, for the good of the social order, to justify failure to serve truth and the actual needs of the Christian conscience. In favour of this could be pleaded the unsettled nature of the times and the anxious pursuit (to some extent legitimate) of security. But this is unacceptable. Every one of us, of course, is guilty of giving way to this temptation, of having regarded the defence of an institution or the past as faithfulness to God, of having identified national, cultural, social or political interests with those of Jesus Christ, or of having allowed faith in him who in fact "emptied himself, taking the form of a servant"[8] to become too closely involved with an established reputation.

Yet no Christian, even one led away by reasoning which causes a mutual hardening of attitudes between groups, can admit on principle that the rule of faith is like this. Nor can he pride himself on a materialism which alienates the Spirit in the "letter", that is, in objective signs and the service of society.

On the other hand, there is a great temptation to withdraw into oneself, to that place constituted by a requirement of conscience. From this inviolable retreat, as from an impregnable stronghold, one feels able to judge all that occurs down on the plain. The great controversies within the Church are regarded as nothing else than political and sordid intrigue. To bear witness to the truth as they see it these prophets come finally to regard themselves as the owners of the truth, without wondering what this legitimate claim is worth beside the immense and immeasurable revelation of God who speaks in so many other experiences. The authentic requirement of conscience incurs the risk that it may set itself apart and become isolated from the God who "emptied himself" in the immense ocean of experiences, whether they were unimportant, anonymous or "traditionalist".

Where the utilitarian thinks only of filling the churches, of strengthening those institutions in danger and of encouraging those scandalized by the innovations of the Spirit, the intransigent takes his own perception of Jesus Christ as his sole criterion; he cuts himself off from his unknown or misunderstood brothers, although many signs, which he rejects, could at least remind him of their existence. What the former rejects as subversive is the

[8] Cf. Phil. 2. 7.

relating of any Christian form of expression to the affirmation, by man, of "the meaning of his own existence".[9] What the latter refuses to accept by rejecting the weight of institutions and the unwieldiness of language, is the resistance of experiences foreign to his own and the means of communication (are there any others beside those which are objective and social?).

The reality is quite unlike this caricature. Any presentation of the problem as a dichotomy rapidly assumes all the disadvantages of a legend. At least, though, it enables the central position dictating the task of each Christian and each Christian group to be described more clearly. " 'Return to me', says the Lord, 'prepare to meet your God.' "[10] This summons is to be heard especially clearly at the present time, with the need to sever socio-cultural attachments so as to include in the building up of the *body* of Christ (that is, of its language) every one of those who bear witness to his Spirit.[11] In addition, there is the need to tolerate, as necessary, those differences which nourish, renew and widen a catholic form of expression, a discourse,[12] defined once and for all by the New Testament as a *connexio oppositorum* that is never closed.[13]

God resists individual experience by the presence of others. General and conciliatory formulations (liturgical, catechetical, theological) encounter the resistance of new and individual experiences provoked by an unwearying God. Under each of these two forms there comes to us an appeal from God. Will it be answered by our seeking protection against him?

[9] Cf. *Gaudium et Spes*, 11, 1; 41, 1; and 44, 1–3. These are passages which connect any gospel and missionary statement with the experience of man which "opens new paths to the truth".

[10] Cf. Amos 4.

[11] Cf. Ephes. 4. 11–16.

[12] *Discurso*, in Spanish, means succession, conjunction and elucidation. On this view the community is *discurso social*; personal progress, in its continuity, is psychological *discurso*. In both cases language is the human focus of experience; it implies divergences (differentials) and on the other hand a necessary relationship between the distinct unities, moments or individuals.

[13] In "Le canon du Nouveau Testament constitue-t-il le fondement de l'unité de l'Église?" (*Exegetische Versuche und Besinnungen*, 1 (Göttingen, 1960), pp. 214–23) E. Käsemann shows that the New Testament is a *complexio oppositorum*. Very rightly Hans Küng quotes the remark, "The Catholic Church is in agreement with the New Testament when it

From the Criticism of Doctrines to the Enigma of Beliefs

To have fixed the limits outside which no unity would be possible and, consequently, no "Christian" communication, means, I think, merely to have recalled the conditions in which the various expressions of faith—liturgical, theological, catechetical or juridical—were drawn up. Detailed treatment must be left to more technical studies.

But in any case this is not to say what the language of unity is or must be today. Nor is it to offer a solution of the major difficulties to which a many-sided undertaking must be adapted. Defects impair and compromise the mutual recognition of the same Lord and the same faith. From among the great number of problems now open for discussion certain more general and more serious questions must at least be uncovered.

The first is in reference to the *critique of ideologies*. Its symptoms are clearly to be discerned in all Western societies. Increasingly crises occur spreading suspicion, a suspicion which raises a subversive question against any theory or proposed course of action—what is there behind this? A kind of discredit or mistrust tends to cause theories to be regarded as relative, especially those thought to be justified in speaking of a truth, or the meaning of history. Because they are seen in connection with the way they operate, their socio-cultural milieu, their utility or their harmfulness, they are no longer believed.[14] This form of criticism does not set up new certainties in opposition to the old. It merely highlights the ambiguous, not to say equivocal, and in any case legendary character of doctrines formulated in a restricted milieu, which are much less "universal" than they claim to be, and which merely reveal the role aspired to by the group from which they originate.

The repercussions and consequences in the Church of this dispute are considerable, since by the same token the discredit of the ideologies calls in question both the truth which is the subject

---

endeavours to gather together the *opposita* (not all, only those which are to be found in the New Testament!) in a valid sense and understand all the New Testament as the Gospel" (*Le Concile épreuve de l'Église* [Paris, 1963], p. 161).

[14] Maurice Montuclard, *Conscience religieuse et démocratie* (Paris, 1963), pp. 201–7.

matter of official pronouncements and the degree to which these pronouncements represent the unity of Christian experiences. These two aspects of the critique are, moreover, connected since any recourse to a *unitary* relation (in the past, for example, Thomism, or natural law or the determination of an "essential") is at the same time actually a claim to define an element without which life and action would no longer be truly Christian. *A blow against unity is a blow against the truth.* Any analysis which reduces a Christian language to the merely local or private category by this very fact forms an attack on its veracity (not its authenticity, which is another question). And so, it is always the purpose of theology to show forth a truth by establishing a unity just as, in the Church's apostolic period, the preaching of Jesus Christ was based on holding all things in common and the formation of a community. The critique of Christian "ideologies" therefore affects the internal structure of faith; it is not enough to oppose it with scorn, denial or condemnation.

But behind this problem facing the meditation and life of the Church there stands another difficulty which is still more fundamental. This is *the riddle of Christian experiences and beliefs.* Recently, a sociologist observed that at the end of the nineteenth century there was considerable disagreement between "doctrines" and "beliefs", that is between official formulations and religious thought or collective Christian experience.[15] More lately still historical, sociological or ethnological studies concerning religious phenomena in the West or in the world[16] continue to emphasize this disagreement. Thus they raise in a more acute way the problem of the relationship between the pronouncements of the *magisterium* or of scholars and expressions of the collective mentality. Gradually these studies are bringing to light what for long has remained concealed by theological or pastoral teaching, or has been forgotten on account of the privileged position of the history of ideas or the formulations drawn up by the "clerisy", namely the great variety to be found in a *different*, puzzling, and often elusive form of Christian life.

It may even be wondered whether this "popular" experience

[15] Cf., for example, M. de Certeau, "Religion et société: les messianismes", in *Études* (April 1969), pp. 608–16.
[16] Cf. John 7.

has hitherto been improperly termed Christian (so that Catholicism would be reduced to the narrow limits of the "cultured" classes in which it can certainly be found), or if Christianity has been wrongly identified with what it meant for the "clergy" (an exceedingly small part in the actual history of the spread of the gospel).

In the past, everything that was not in agreement with the teaching of the *magisterium* was classed as "ignorance", "superstition" or even as "heresy". This state of absolute certainty is now wavering. An unknown world stands before us, which calls itself Christian and yet is quite unlike our picture of what Christian is: "another country", one that is huge and many-sided beneath the forms of expression (whether missionary or theological) which concealed it. We clergy cannot get rid of this great mass of people, nor consider ourselves qualified to represent it nor even claim any identity with it. Dogmatic imperialism, no more than the feigning of a certain solidarity, is no answer to the question raised by so many voices now beginning to be heard. Thus the relationship between official statements about faith and the actual experience of faith indeed becomes problematic.

Yet one postulate that cannot be dissociated from faith provides us with a principle of solution on the basis of which the problem might be solved. For what causes the problem is, in the last analysis, the mystery of the presence of God hidden in these experiences. In fact, what we have here, though out of context, is the traditional statement of Christian theology about the "analogical" nature of any statement about God. For a long time all theological statements have had to admit this. For example, it is true that God is "good" or "personal", but in another respect it is untrue. The weight of his transcendence makes any proposition relative, even to the point that the statement "God exists" has to be followed by a denial. Perhaps the puzzling relationship between official formulations and actual experience belongs to the same order. Perhaps the fact that pronouncements of the *magisterium* are made relative by the immense extent of popular piety belongs to the mystery of the experience of God. This mystery, of course, must be expressed, but it goes far beyond and negates, by disputing it, any statement. Perhaps in the mode of this confrontation of their "reason" (inspired by faith) and the popular religious "sense" (also inspired by faith) the theologians find themselves once more in the presence of their judge, the living God found in the hearts of men.

The Making of Unity

From different angles we are constantly sent back from unity to the truth and conversely. A language of unity is necessary for the manifestation of revealed truth, but the deficiencies and gaps in this language remind us with what truth we are concerned in any affirmation of faith.

In view of the impossibility of settling here the tasks to which the Christian community is once again called by its faith, at least it must be repeated that this faith implies the necessary connection between personal requirement and communication, or between experience of the Absolute and social language. Where this assurance is lacking there no longer exists, I consider, any Christian faith founded on God incarnate. This will help us to establish certain principles and tendencies.

1. Unity is never *given*. It belongs to the spiritual order, based on faith in God, and at the same time it cannot be dissociated from history, that is, from a state of development. If the "structure" or logic of faith was established once for all with the apostolic conjunction of the presence (of Jesus) and the (ecclesial) community, if the first Christian language (of the New Testament) defines and postulates this conjunction as the "rule of faith", this inaugurates a task which needs to be resumed progressively as history is renewed, even if this task always follows the same pattern in direct relation with the same Spirit.

2. The first consequence of this is that Christian language would cease to proclaim the Truth if it abolished the right of every Christian conscience to express itself, to have a place in the language of the community or to make itself heard—a right granted not merely in the name of goodwill, but in the name of a Truth that is also affirmed by all that is irrecusable and immutable in the conscience of a man and a Christian.

3. A further consequence is the impossibility for the individual to set up his private experience, however profound, as the rule of faith and standard of truth. Only too often nowadays, due to the inevitable reasoning arising from present tensions, we find

certain demands of the gospel, hitherto misunderstood or unknown, incapable of bearing witness save by claiming to be the only one or by wishing to absorb all others.

4. In this respect in the whole ecclesial community, as in each group, the resistance of others means a *call to conversion*. It is always a formidable confrontation for it is God with whom we are face to face (as it was with the Pharisees so "faithful" to Moses, the Law and God).[17] God in the likeness of man. He is the Stranger. He brings us a truth from which we cannot be separated and which we are always in danger of failing to accept because of our reliance on knowledge or experiences already held as "true".

5. In short, the same holds for unity, and therefore for its expression, as for truth: it must be achieved and put into practice. "He who does what is true", said Jesus, "comes to the light." This can be interpreted as, "He who makes unity finds the truth", and it is probably the stimulus of this truth which provokes in us the desire for unity. Resort to the demands of conscience conditions the truth of the communication and prevents us being deceived by the hypocrisy always latent within us. But recourse to the desire for unity, and to the "poverty" which makes others indispensable to us, also drives out the personal or collective "sufficiency" of localized, and in the last resort, idolatrous truths. Thus the development, the formulation of unity continues like a progress forward, rather than rotation round a centre. Its language, the living principle of which, given once for all, is the Spirit who is received in tongues of fire by each of the members of the same community. But there is never an end to God's dealings with us.

[17] Cf. John 3. 21; *poiein ten aletheian* ("do what is true") is a phrase used six or seven times in the Old Testament to designate someone who acts straightforwardly or faithfully. In St John there is a closer connection between *decision* and *truth. Poiein* means both *produce* (unlike *pratein* which insists on the agent of the action, while *poiein* points rather to its result; it is also the biblical word for the creation in the Septuagint) and *translate into action* (to act according to the truth, which "springs from the heart"). "Faithfulness" refers to a more fundamental indwelling of the truth.

Translated by Lancelot Sheppard

Carlos-Josaphat Pinto de Oliveira

The Church, Orthodoxy and a Pluralist Society

GREAT strides are now being made in the Church's theological awareness of her own nature. She sees herself as the mysterious centre of time and space in which the Word is effectively proclaimed and saving grace is at work. A whole series of factors characterizes this new and widespread awareness. It is a fruitful stimulus to theology and it has also had some effect on the attitudes of the *magisterium*. Vatican II was the official expression of these fresh insights, and in more than one respect its inspiration.

Yet, as in other comparable periods, such progress runs the danger of being compromised or impeded by recessive elements. Among these, the most powerful is the concept of orthodoxy and the role claimed by the Church as its protector—orthodoxy being seen in the largely static terms of a "deposit". Despite opting for dialogue and the abandonment of repressive or negative controls,[1] an atmosphere of uncertainty will continue as long as a narrow idea of orthodoxy connected with the outdated concept of monolithic Christendom persists.

Surely theology could encourage the mature growth of the Christian consciousness, and serve the *magisterium*, by deepening the whole conception of faith, especially to the extent that this latter represents a unique form of knowledge? Continuing theological investigation would form an opportune extension of the ecclesiological studies that prepared the way for the most liberal

[1] I am thinking, for example, of the Encyclical *Ecclesiam suam* and the Motu proprio *Integrae servandae* (7 Dec. 1965) announcing the reform of the Holy Office.

and beneficial of the Council's achievements. It must not evade the two fundamental aspects of the problem—first, to face squarely the actual situation of orthodoxy in a pluralist world, and then to try to discover the form that would enable it to remain faithful to the theological nature of faith, rather than to certain virtually juridical measures still favoured on occasion by some ecclesiastics.

I. Characteristics and Questions of a Pluralist Society

I shall begin with the semantic aspects and then examine the questions raised by pluralism in the pursuit of orthodoxy in the modern world.

1. *Two Principal Senses of Pluralism*

Even at the risk of too schematic a treatment or of undue emphasis on certain points, it seems preferable to define pluralism in the present context. Leaving aside the diversity of institutions, and the social differentiation of groups and customs, I shall consider here only the heterogeneity of ideas and theories, to the extent that they affect the theme of this paper. There is a twofold meaning to be discerned; the essential difference depends on the depth indicated by the term pluralism: namely, the communication *or* the fundamental significance of faith itself.

(*a*) Theological Pluralism

Theological pluralism refers to the formulation at different doctrinal or intellectual levels of a particular human, ethical, religious or theological experience. The difference of expression will derive from the diversity of the cultural milieu but will express the evolution of a fundamentally identical spiritual life. In Christian tradition it is concerned principally with the theological homogeneity of faith, given expression through the use of religious, dogmatic or theological means of communication and drawing on cultural, philosophical and artistic materials of a very varied and sometimes anomalous nature.

Thus we can understand the agreement—but without any compromise or compounding—revealed by a comparison of the syntheses of, say, St Thomas and St Augustine, especially in the field of anthropology or ethics. In a realist theology, thanks to "concepts" and "natures" taken from an ontology based on the consistency of "being" and "physis", Aquinas was able to transcribe the traditional data which the Augustinian school expressed in a predominantly symbolist anthropology, founded on the distinction between *res* and *signa*. This theological method claimed to remain faithful not only to biblical revelation but to its patristic expression, an assertion that the history of dogma appears in the main to uphold.

An even more striking example can be found in the New Testament where consideration of the christological mystery appears to assume a successive or concomitant diversity of images and ideas which none the less show clearly the continuance throughout of a fundamental twofold theme: the Son of Man in his humility and exaltation, the suffering Servant and the Lord of glory, Jesus of Nazareth becoming Christ, the Saviour and the Judge. Divine transcendence and human abasement are indissociable in Christ. In this case the term plurality might be more appropriate than pluralism.

(*b*) PLURALISM IN THE PERCEPTION OF FAITH AND VALUES

Pluralism can denote a far greater divergence: the co-existence of systems of life and thought possessing conflicting assessments of the principles held by either side as fundamental, or the understanding of certain values also regarded as fundamental.

This appears to be the case, for example, with the Christian or Marxist view of the world, despite the possibilities of collaboration between believers and atheists. Catholic and Protestant ideas on the *magisterium* at work in the Church are another instance of the same thing; and the opposition between them at the doctrinal level becomes progressively sharper as the growing ecumenical dialogue reveals the points at issue. It is not a straightforward question of divergence, as the term pluralism might seem to imply. The agreement is fundamental, though latent or implicit. It is probably this encounter, in life or work, that is designated by terms like "world" or "society", when qualified as "pluralist". A certain mutual agreement is required in order to live together in the same human society. Some similarity of views and preferences is indispensable in concrete reality. Precisely implicit agreement enables dialogue to take place. It implies not merely tolerance or a presumption of good faith in both of those who want to bring the other round to their own point of view in the end. The real basis of dialogue is the certainty that implicit experience is more important than explicit formulation. The living presence of the truth inspiring the co-existence and action of men separated ideologically or doctrinally is the positive reality of pluralism, which is not just an evil to be tolerated. It stands for a productive and stimulating aspect of the human condition, and especially of the people of God as they progress towards the "fullness of truth" under the guidance of the Spirit (cf. John 16. 13). Of course pluralism which implies disagreement and even dissension, especially among believers, is a great misfortune. It is a reminder, very often, of the limitations of the human mind and still more of the darkness and the impediments caused by sin. Nevertheless, the final explanation of the pluralist state is to be found in the eschatological character of salvation—the fullness of the divine mysteries, which in every age are greater than history and demand scrutiny by all in the certainty that the Spirit of truth will be the cause of an experience in the inmost hearts of men and in communities; this experience is far richer than all dogmatic formulations, however well adapted they may be. This characterizes the pluralism which dialogue between believers, and even between men of good will, has caused to find favour in the Church since the accession of John XXIII, and especially since Vatican II. But this phenomenon, with all its spiritual advantages, has to be faced with the correlative conception of orthodoxy, which does not appear to have made corresponding progress.

2. *The Advent of Pluralism and the Pursuit of Orthodoxy*

I intend to confront the pluralism, as it is at present, in its twofold significance, with the maintenance and perfecting of orthodoxy which seems a fundamental mission of the Church—especially of its supreme authority exercised by the episcopal body under the leadership of the Pope.

In harmony with the first meaning of pluralism Vatican II seems to require a theological pluralism in the Church. Some documents appear to say so explicitly (cf. the Decree on Ecumenism, n. 4, 10–11); but more particularly the underlying truth, of course, is witnessed to in biblical and traditional texts; and it is served by dogmatic formulations; but it is only to be found dwelling in the mind of the believer enlightened by the Spirit. This historical and living presence of the truth is expressed in a diffuse and even divergent manner; this divergence can be made more acute and the divisions of philosophical or religious systems more clear-cut. But to do so would amount to a failure to understand man and the human condition in their universal implications and faltering attempts to advance. For the Christian, indeed, it would mean blindness to the Spirit of truth at work in men's hearts and communities, leading them to unity in their recognition of the Mystery that transcends all systematic formulation.

The fundamental question facing us is this: How could an expression of orthodoxy serve the living truth, the Spirit at work today in the world?

II. Orthodoxy: Inevitable Tension

In Christian tradition, probably more acutely than in any other religious movement, there is a tendency towards the establishment of a rule of orthodoxy. Primarily it is intended as the precise doctrinal expression of the whole of revealed knowledge forming the object of faith of the whole of the people of God today (taking into account its progress in history). It seeks a form of expression that will allow its "profession" in the hearts of believers, and the proclamation of the message to the world. The most authentic form of inspiration leading to the formulation of an orthodoxy is the affirmation of "catholicity"; of universality in relation to the content of the Word, the body of believers and the historical development of human communication.

1. *Definition and Universality*

In the history of orthodoxy there has been a continual tension between this effort at determination and the infinite range of the divine word which faith desires to receive and proclaim. Three aspects of this tension can be distinguished. Firstly, in the realm of the mind, a dogma, for example, the most typical manifestation of orthodoxy, is intended as the considered doctrinal expression of a truth, through the medium of the culture of a period, but in relation to the universality of the human mind, and still more to the infinite nature of the meaning of the divine word itself.

The Catholic dogmatic system, especially since the Council of Trent, while preaching this universality of the formulas of faith and denying their encapsulation in a particular system of thought, has been clothed in the language of scholastic theology. But the philosophy of the Schools cannot lay claim to the universality of the mind in quest of truth through different cultures and historical situations, and therefore represents a limitation. It even becomes a greater hindrance to universal communication, by persisting in its unconscious assumption that it is the crystal-clear language of revealed truth, and in natural affinity with it.

There is a further aspect to this tension: dogmatic formulation is intended to encourage the life of faith of the people of God, yet frequently reflects the controversies of a particular period. It was drawn up as a defence against heresy. It has taken one element in isolation, and thus become particularized; it no longer corresponds with the full meaning of the Word of God, which causes the "righteous man to live by faith". The same tension also occurs in the context of the action of the Spirit among the people of God as a whole, as they help the *magisterium* to activate and renew Christian life. Because the *magisterium* is inclined to see fidelity to orthodoxy as an attachment to already established formulas, and refers only to its own statements (without regard to the questionings and vitality of the ecclesial body as a whole), a disquieting situation could arise. Initially, it would be attributable to this incomplete idea of the sources of orthodox faith.

2. *Inflexibility or Dissolution*

Here there is a real danger, that is the greater since, unlike mere tensions, it affects something precious—the faith of the people of God.

The first risk is precisely what might be called the "heresy of orthodoxy": reliance on the established positions of the past and the repetition of traditional formulas. It means keeping—for the sake of safety at the present time—what has been determined in the past, without taking account of the possible gap between two phases of intellectual development, or without taking seriously qualitatively different stages in the history of culture. Connected with this unyielding attitude is a reduction to the same level of the propositions of faith, expressed so that the articles of the creed lose their order of importance and seem to be flattened out in a system of linear affirmations.

This attitude, which renders any ecumenical dialogue sterile, Vatican II wished to exclude by calling on Christians to rediscover the hierarchy of the divine mysteries (cf. Decree on Ecumenism, 2, n. 11). To seek to emphasize those elements which are held as "typically Catholic", that is, those which have been drawn up in opposition to heresies, is a clear instance of the narrowness in question. It would amount to upsetting the balance of the message of salvation, were the harmony of the kerygma upset for the sake of what proved eventually to be mere accidental developments.

On the other hand, one cause of this so-called narrow orthodox view is a danger which must not be concealed; it is a dissolution of the content of faith; a removal of any sense of truth and a reduction to a point of view which, while claiming to be effective, is blind.

Since the advent of the modern world and the progress of scientific knowledge, some theologians have been driven to characterize the "night of faith" not by the lack of evidence, but—radically—by an absence of intellectual content. To avoid this deviation, which in its extreme form would prevent any proclamation of the message, but also to check any tendency to a narrow position which would only serve to compromise it, the Church today must undertake a thorough appraisal of its conception of orthodoxy, and bring its doctrinal and pastoral practice into line with it.

III. Mission of the Church and a Profounder View of Orthodoxy

Any progress in the attitude of the Church (i.e. of the people of God guided by the hierarchy, in the face of the problems raised by the pluralism of the modern world) is immediately and directly dependent on a deeper view of faith. A theology meditating on the life of the Church (the Church preaches "what she believes, what she is", cf. Constitution *Dei Verbum*, 2, n. 8) requires that we consider the elements assumed by the attitude of the Church towards the word of God today; and also that these elements should be arranged according to their intrinsic hierarchy, that is, in relation to the central event of salvation as proclaimed in the New Testament kerygma and received by the body of believers as a whole.

1. *Integral Vision of Faith, the Foundation of Orthodoxy*

There is obviously a relationship between the historical forms of orthodoxy and the idea of faith as formulated, but more especially as lived by the Church, and particularly by those who are responsible for her *magisterium*. The advance achieved by the last Council in its definition of faith, and still more by the living notion underlying the more characteristic attitudes adopted, enables us to hope for and to strive to seek a more adequate and comprehensive form of orthodoxy.

Whereas Vatican I emphasized the intellectual aspects of faith, Vatican II defined it as the complete homage of the whole man in submission to God and responding to his word revealed in the history of salvation (Constitution *Dei Verbum*, 1, n. 5). This word was uttered in a perfect manner in the revelation of Jesus Christ. But it is made real and reveals its full meaning of truth and salvation "now", because God who has spoken through his Son is in communication at every moment of history with the Church —his people—by means of the enlightening and vivifying action of the Spirit (cf. *Dei Verbum* 2, n. 8). Faith is therefore of the same dimension as the Word, and unfolds its meanings in history. This idea of faith is the inspiration of the relationships which the Church wants to have with the world, in accordance with the Constitution *Gaudium et Spes*, and the attitude of respect that she feels called to show towards the non-Catholic Christian communities and non-Christian religions. A similar view of faith derives from a new type of orthodoxy—that which seeks to grasp the meaning of the word of God in pluralism.

2. *In Face of Pluralism*

The Church stands guarantor that God speaks today in history through a variety of languages and many kinds of human experience. In a world in which desires for justice, brotherhood, communications between men and peoples are keenly felt, the Church shows the harmony of these values with the universal *Agape* revealed in the words, life and—especially—death of Christ.

The narrow pursuit of orthodoxy led to churchmen lacking all understanding of the rights of man and the ideals of freedom in the nineteenth century.[2] On the other hand, faithful to the power of the living word of God, the Church shows the way to unity not in the monotonous repetition of certain formulas, but by calling for and encouraging the pursuit of a harmony that is realized at the different levels of human communication. The richness, transcendence and fruitfulness of the word of God are capable of expression in a certain dogmatic pluralism or, more correctly, in a plurality of dogmatic expressions, under the authority of the *magisterium* and through a living exchange with the community of believers.

Conclusion

A new form of positive and dynamic orthodoxy is taking shape in the Church—though somewhat laboriously on occasion. It is appropriate in an "open society", just as the type of orthodoxy that went with the Inquisition and the Holy Office belonged to a "closed society" (in H. Bergson's sense). This view of orthodoxy forms part of an ecclesial dialogue; in it, the teaching of the Church is given as a living word, a conversation of the whole Church, really attentive to the historical period through which the world is passing. This teaching is developed in three stages: the preparation, the promulgation and the results of doctrinal pronouncements. This does not mean that the authority of the magisterial documents is derived from the subsequent approbation of the whole body of the Church; that would imply a return to the old Gallican error. But their significance in the life of the faithful and the world today is revealed only by means of the living dialogue in which the decrees of the pontifical and episcopal *magisterium*, the theological reflection and the participation of the people of God (contributing their own typical experience) are really active and co-ordinated.

[2] For the documentation and the various shades of meaning to be applied to this assertion, see C. J. Pinto de Oliveira, O.P., *Information et Propagande, Responsabilité chrétiennes* (Paris, 1968), Chapter II, pp. 53–108.

Can we already discern the lines that the development of this open and dynamic orthodoxy will follow? Unless some lack of courage or vision compromises its development, it will try to apprehend the fundamental ideas of the word of God in their totality, while following the different forms of their biblical and traditional expression. It will take into account the hierarchy of divine mysteries as well as the elements of Christian life, rather than an entirely material attachment to the actual dogmatic formulations that historical vicissitudes, or opposition to heretics, made necessary in certain epochs of Christian history. Further, bearing in mind the variety of levels of human communication used by revelation and tradition, it will take care, because of its concern for fidelity, to avoid uniformity in formulas whenever the variety of situations, regions and cultures requires plurality for the benefit of the transcendent unity of the divine word under the action of the Holy Spirit.

But principally the active faith of the people of God and the mission of the *magisterium* are called to fulfil a prophetic function as hearers—a function, indeed, which seems a trial, and a task that is never completed. It is a matter of paying heed to the tendencies (sometimes scarcely outlined or expressed in different ways), and to the human values at work in the world (often only glimpsed partially), in order to confront them with the central event constituted by the love of God given and revealed in Jesus Christ. Under this inspiration—which becomes also a sovereign requirement of profound and effective affinity with the word of God—the Church will be in a position to discern the constants in a variety of statements, and the harmony in religious or cultural plurality. This prophetic insight would not impede the task of assisting the development of seminal truths, and the broadening of incomplete expressions; that is, would not block the rectification from within of inadequate formulations.

Translated by Lancelot Sheppard

PART II
BULLETIN

Wolfgang Dietzfelbinger

"Revivalist" Tendencies in the German Evangelical Church

FOR some years now various West German Evangelicals have repeatedly expressed their deep-felt concern about the way things are going in theology and in the Church itself. At first these were individual plaints, but recently there has been a tendency among critics to organize themselves in more formal groups. The following movements have achieved the greatest prominence: the "*Kein anderes Evangelium*", or "No Other Gospel" group (taking its name from Galatians I. 6), the "*Sammlung um Bibel und Bekenntnis*", or "Scriptural and Confessing Assembly", and—in Württemberg—the "*Ludwig-Hofacker-Vereinigung*", or "Ludwig Hofacker Union". There are no absolutely clear boundaries between these alliances and other related groups. Occasionally people are members of more than one organization; there are frequent exchanges of speakers, activities and demonstrations in common, and various forms of intercommunication. Their adherents are all members of the Evangelical Church, and are for the most part ministers actively engaged in parish work or preaching, although some are academics; laymen also belong to these "revivalist" groups. No exact statistics are available since there is no rigidly conducted, exclusive organization, but a core of immediately responsible co-workers at the centre of a widening circle of friends, sympathizers and interested parties, among whom the degrees of adherence are so various that no precise estimate is possible.

These groups make their views known in different ways. There have been scholarly discussions with professors of theology and bishops; public statements and near-demonstrations; and a flood of indignant letters to the representatives of modern theology. Church papers and magazines, the dailies and other mass communications media have served as channels of this particular form of protest. There has been an avalanche of apologetical and polemical leaflets, pamphlets, journals and small-format paperbacks. The very variety of these manifestations of dissent is some indication that the struggle for pure faith and doctrine (allegedly universally threatened) draws its supporters from quite different levels of the Church. But all seem of one conviction in determining the sources of the threat to the "old faith": such are the so-called "existential" theology whose origins are linked with the name of Rudolf Bultmann, and the secularization of the Church in its relation to the world and to morals, which is seen as closely bound up with existential theology.

I. Scripture

The above-mentioned groups raise a considerable number of objections against existential theology. They claim that historical and critical scholarship has made the factuality of central events in the story of salvation appear questionable, and made church-people uncertain about their reality; that such efforts no longer allow any room for acceptance of Jesus' birth from a virgin, and of his miracles, resurrection and ascension; that Jesus has been degraded to become a mere human being, an exemplar of love and a teacher of morals, while his atoning death and effective victory over dissolution have been removed from the area of debate. Further, they assert that God himself is no longer understood in a personal sense, thus ridding prayer of any recipient; that eschatology is reduced to the attainment of proficient self-understanding in the present, thus losing its apocalyptic reference to the future; that, as a result of making absolute theological distinctions between the individual authors of the Bible, the common witness of the New Testament has been surrendered; and that simultaneously the unique basis for any ecclesiology has disappeared, since when the Bible is understood thus, the Church can manifest itself only indeterminately. They deplore the dismissal of divine transcendence and the restriction of the gospel to an immanent range of reference, and trace the source of the general malady to a conscious or unconscious interpretation of the Bible according to the preconceptions of existential philosophy.

This last objection raised by the revivalists leads one to expect in their literature some mention of the extent to which the assumptions of existential philosophy are inappropriate to the Bible, or at least an explanation of what they would consider to be valid presuppositions for an encounter with Holy Writ. One's expectations are disappointed. The revivalist literature in question contains no thought about specific hermeneutical methods. For them the "what" of proclamation is disproportionately more important than its "how"; content means everything, whereas *form* is almost wholly without import. Any questions about the assumptions that are needed to tackle the matter are answered with the matter itself.

This process is itself based on an assumption that the Bible ought to come across without any human bias to the message. Of course there is a basic short-circuiting of thought here, which seems all the more culpable when the history of theology shows that there never has been (and therefore never will be) any biblical studies totally without initial assumptions and qualifications. Every student and interpreter of the Bible approaches it with definite presuppositions, and reads it with the aid of a pair of mental spectacles. The pronouncements of the revivalists are only further confirmations of this truth of experience.

In such key-words of their literature as "children of God", "true Christians", "resurrected Christians", "convert", "devout of heart", "total surrender", the initiated will recognize at once that the Bible is being interpreted according to the preconceptions of an unbroken pietism. It is a pietism marked by the traits of an individualistic psychology; a faith which sees everything as amounting to the resurrection of the individual, and the assembly of the resurrected individuals within a small group. In comparison with this overriding consideration all such problems of the institutional Church as the question of office, the sacraments, written professions of faith and confessional emphasis are wholly subordinate. These problems are subject to attitudes ranging from well-meaning though uninterested tolerance to open mistrust. Such tendencies are apparent in the case of the "No Other Gospel" group, which belongs to the "confessing" tradition. No-Other-Gospellers make use of an additional hermeneutical key to the truth, in the shape of traditional Church dogma—i.e., the Apostles' Creed. This means that they tend to affect a style more heavily laced with philosophical and traditional dogmatic terms than is apparent in the language of pietism pure and simple. Together with "son of God", "soul", "original sin", we get words like "transcendence", "ontology", "person", "history", "nothingness" used as interpretative counters requiring no additional precise explanation or qualification.

The "No Other Gospel" group understands by the notion of "confession" the act of profession (*confessio qua*), whereas the "Scriptural and Confessing Assembly" takes it to mean the content (*confessio quae*) of the Lutheran confessional writings. This content includes, say, an emphasis on the real presence of Christ in the Lord's Supper or on the ministry (usually with a decided rejection of the ordination of women). For this Lutheran group the most obvious source of epistemological assumptions is the individual conscience. Of course, the question of the attachment of the confessional writings to a particular era is not raised; there is no consideration at all of the fact that they can be read in a very different sense according to whether they are interpreted by Luther, by Melanchthon, by orthodox Lutheranism, or by the "new" Lutheranism of the nineteenth century—to say nothing of more recent exegesis.

The difference between the revivalist groups and existential theology is not so much to be found in the distinction between an unconditioned and a definite method of understanding the Bible. There are certain preconceptions on both sides, but in the one case they are more emphatically practical in the ecclesiastical sense, and for the most part accepted without critical analysis, whereas in the other they are largely philosophical and more obviously consciously developed. If it were really possible to use this as an acceptable basis for study of the two sides, it would offer an adequate beginning for a critical comparative examination of their specific notions and a test of their utility. Unfortunately, however, the revivalist groups have hardly as yet attained to the necessary degree of conscious reflection; and so, instead of achieving an almost scientific confrontation, one is reduced to a fruitless, superficially far-ranging though actually repetitious cross-purpose polemicism.

II. Anthropology

A similar result is achieved in any inquiry after the dominant conception of man in each case. In general the attack on existential theology asserts that its supporters are lacking in sincerity and serious commitment. There is no acknowledgment of the fact that this theology was developed with the eminently practical intention of preaching the gospel in a way appropriate to twentieth-century man. The objection raised is that this kind of concern for humankind goes too far when it reduces or falsifies the gospel for their sake, merely selecting what modern man is ready to accept but hushing up the *skandalon* of the Christian message, and thus turning theology into anthropology.

The man who switches on an electric light or listens to a wireless set cannot simultaneously be a believer in the New Testament world of spirits and miracles; this has been offered as a convenient formulation of the picture of man afforded by existential theology. The revivalist groups have launched their attacks against it on two levels. An attempt has been made to show that the background of this conception of man has already been superseded by the latest developments in the natural sciences. Various well-known physicists are cited to show the restricted validity of causality and the limitations of human cognition. When the miracles are then conveniently located in this space beyond man's comprehension, one has the impression that God, "for whom all things are possible", is rather too easily and strictly forced to assume the role of stopgap for the inexplicable, without any greater degree of probability that the inexplicable in question will have any part to play in this my life. And of course the logical connection between possibility and factual occurrence is missing.

Another attempt is made to weaken the anthropology of existential theology by citing instances in which the "old faith" has proved effective for men of the present, from the conversion of an alcoholic all the way to the mass profession of twenty thousand faithful at the Dortmund *Bekenntnisversammlung* in 1966.

These efforts can provide a corrective for the human image of existential theology, which is heavily intellectualized. They do force one to remember that human faith is not influenced by reason alone, but comprises areas which lie beyond the sway of the *ratio*, and which come within the competence of the practical cure of souls. Here the arguments of the groups whose members are largely engaged in the active ministry are quite persuasive.

Nevertheless, this corrective does not refute the picture of man it seeks to criticize. What it does show is that there are men alive today for whom Scripture as it is offers no intellectual difficulties: not because they are expressly prepared to make a *sacrificium intellectus*, but because in their case—for the most part—other levels of the person are affected. But of course there is also the first-mentioned type who *is* exposed to such difficulties, remains indifferent to traditional formulas, and can be reached only by a new form of proclamation of the gospel. Here one might well set credit balance against credit balance. But in no case is there any justification for automatically equating intellectual opposition (the character of which certainly requires examination) with refusal of the Christian *skandalon*. But because this does happen in the revivalist groups, with a simultaneous absolutization of the human type that makes them up, any discussion of the nature of present-day man is doomed before it has properly started.

III. Profile

The more one studies the revivalist groups, the more one is forced to ask if they are basically concerned with mere defensiveness against danger or if there is also some original theological conception at their root. In several series of publications in the last few years, the individual understanding of faith has been pushed hard together with occasional refutations of any teaching to the contrary. These documents are always short and inadequate. On the other hand, they do not restrict themselves to the examination of a single point of belief, but survey the whole content of faith from prolegomena to eschatology. In general such publications are intended for all levels of the community and therefore have to be easily comprehensible.

All these factors have an inevitable result: the ultimate product of these pamphlets is so unnuanced and curtailed that for the most part it does not really touch on existential theology at all; indeed, they are so phrased that (when the appropriate interpretation is supplied) existential theologians could even give their assent to the pronouncements as made. The actual anathemata on the other hand are basically what such things have always been: the teaching under attack is apostrophized not in its essence but in inessentials, themselves on occasion desubtilized and caricatured. The end result is somewhat surprising: the emphasis is to all intents and purposes much more clearly placed not on the differences that might well be stressed between the confessing movement and existential theology, but on the relationship between them. This impression is heightened by the realization that to a considerable extent both parties have recourse to the same authorities of the past. Of course in both cases the Bible is the favourite source of citations. After that, the revivalists tend to quote Luther—but Luther also happens to figure pretty frequently as a star witness for existential theology. Adolf Schlatter is also called in as a supporter of the "old faith"; but then it was Ernst Käsemann—Bultmann's disciple of all people—who effected a Schlatter renaissance in New Testament scholarship.

Naturally the revivalist groups object to this kind of judgment, and claim that although the same terminology is used on both sides it means something very different in each case. Existential theologians—consciously or unconsciously—are said to make confrontation all the more difficult by using traditional terms in senses contrary to their original connotations. They use the word "God", but (so it is asserted) by it they mean the very ground of being, or a certain form of common humanity; they speak of "justification", "resurrection", "grace" and the "Holy Spirit", and really all they are talking about is the new "self-awareness"; they refer to "prayer", and all they have in mind is "meditation". In this way existential theologians are accused of reducing traditional concepts to empty or indeterminately filled husks—mere cyphers and labels without any, or with a totally different content.

These assertions have to be countered with the question whether existential theology (from the viewpoint for once of material findings) is not basically justified in seeking for a new interpretation of traditional notions. On looking back at the history of even one theological concept, it soon becomes clear that its meaning has changed time and time again. As far as contemporary usage is concerned, this means either that—for plausible reasons—I have recourse to a meaning that the term in question once had, or that I try to find a specific meaning that seems pertinent today. For example, in the case of the word "person", it is sensible to ask whether it should be understood as traditional dogma understood it, or according to the usage of idealism, or that of romanticism. But here the revivalist groups provide no answer. They believe that they know what the terms denote, without any need for close inquiry. They predetermine a meaning without allowing it any clarification. They are pure revivalists in the sense that they restrict themselves to terminology from the "faith of the Fathers" which is supposed to imply a kind of normative understanding demanding no further inquiry.

The salient built up against existential theology therefore has no specific theological design. Consequently the historical character of the individual groups (already characterized as pietism, revivalism and orthodox Lutheranism) is the more apparent. It must be remembered that these tendencies are actually quite opposed to one another, and it is a matter for conjecture how firm the alliance between them really is, and how long it can last. The continuance of the groups in question seems anything but guaranteed if one looks at the often extreme distance between the specific positions of their individual members. At the one extreme there is the confirmed Lutheran of the Scandinavian High Church movement, and at the other the Württemberg Pietist who would find the least trace of a Catholicizing tendency highly suspect. Uneasy neighbours are the part-time lay preacher, for whom the invisible and charismatic action of the Holy Spirit is the whole matter, and the "Assembly" man who jealously preserves a genuine sacramental consciousness. The question is inevitable: What bond can effectively secure this union between the disparate currents of orthodoxy and pietism?

IV. Prospects

Undeniably the German Evangelical Church is in a state of crisis. The revivalist groups perform a service in firmly calling attention to this crisis. But the methods chosen—jeremiads and prophecies of disaster—are inappropriate. The crisis is a crisis of growth. Certainly existential theology has played a decisive role in it. This is not the place to determine how far its function might justly be called inspiring and beneficial, restrictive or curative, productive of improvement or destructive, quite apart from the fact that this theology itself has the most varied tributaries and affords currents of energy which fully acknowledge their responsibility to and for the Church, as well as those which lack such responsibility. In any case, the situation that has resulted is such that it must be confronted in its essentials by anyone who seeks to co-operate in the management of the crisis.

It should now be clear that the revivalist groups have taken only a very inadequate part in this confrontation. The most emphatic tendency is that of assuming the role of *beatus possidens*, and feeling that they are representatives of the only true Church. They have challenged Church leaders, and feel themselves called to initiate proceedings against heretics, and to refuse academic credits to theology students for attending the lectures of certain professors. They have urged sympathetic parishioners to shun the services of certain ministers and to keep their children away from religious instruction given by such suspect pastors. They have condemned dialogues with modern theologians as "controversial theology"; and two churches are already known to have been formed on the actual basis of this resistance alone.

The revivalist groups would justify these tendencies from responsibility for doctrine and the faithful. I would prefer to see them as definite trends towards schism, which fortunately have to date been voiced only sporadically and in a comparatively muted fashion. There is the danger that a still sound core of the Church (to the extent that it actually is sound!) could in the future be adversely affected by this particular crisis; and also the danger that the Church might forget its particular commission and adapt itself wholly to the world. But there is no point in grappling with such a threat by means of the contrary errors of sheer reaction. Pure rejection and opposition could eventually result in an ecclesiastical group being united and inward-looking, but thereby taking on the character of a sect sealed off from the outside world. Such a sect could sing its own praises for preserving its salt from losing its savour; but with just as disastrous a consequence as a loss of savour—never being allowed to touch the food it's supposed to spice.

It is impossible to turn back the wheel of history, or the wheel of spiritual and theological history—whether it is seen as beneficial or disastrous. The Church cannot take refuge in yesteryear and behave as if nothing had happened in the meantime. She ought to and must unremittingly make creative use of the rich inheritance afforded her by her tradition, thus making advantage of the experiences of the Fathers and avoiding the wrong tracks followed by earlier prospectors. She must never accept the past indeterminately and without analysis, but must incur her responsibility to it in full consciousness of what was and is being done with it.

Of course there must be limits. But one's impression is that the decisive boundaries are still not clearly marked out. In any case, their nature is certainly such that peremptory theses and refutations are quite inappropriate. Nowadays a coarse sieve is no use at all for sifting the chaff from the grain. Anyway, how far can this kind of separation work be deemed a human function at all? There is a lot of disaffection, confusion, recklessness, irresponsibility and even near-infamy within the Evangelical Church today. But do short-circuit condemnations or uncritical alliances offer the only alternative? Isn't there a form of action which might be characterized as patient observation, which attentively traces the course of development, making its own contribution and donating its own stimulus in one case, carefully exerting some braking power and issuing a challenge in another? It could be branded as "tactics" or "indecisiveness", but it might also be seen as a course of action characterized by reliance on the Holy Spirit, who in his own time will have the unhealthy decay, the extreme perish, the unfruitful come to growth, and life for the future evolve out of the travail of the present.

These few reflections should give some indication of the future prospects for the "revivalist" groups. They are not free from the dangers of self-isolation and being left behind on the more conservative side of the road the Church must travel. On the other hand, they are open to the possibility of becoming flexible and proficient partners in dialogue within the Evangelical Church, and thus serving it beneficially.

RELEVANT LITERATURE

Gerhard Bergmann, *Kirche am Scheideweg*, Schriftenmissionsverlag Gladbeck (1967); Otto Rodenberg, *Der Weg Gottes*, Brockhaus Wuppertal (1968); Sven Findeisen, Helmuth Frey, Wilhelm Johanning, *Das Kreuz Jesu und die Krise der Evangelischen Kirche*, Liebenzeller Studienhefte 5 (1967); Georg Huntemann, *Angriff auf die Moderne*, Brockhaus Wuppertal (1966); Walter Kunneth, *Von Gott Reden?*, Brockhaus Wuppertal (1965); Walter Kunneth, *Dimensionen des Glaubens*, Steinkopf Stuttgart (1967); Günter Klein, Walter Kunneth, *Bekenntnis im Widerstreit*, Mohn Gütersloh (1967); Peter Hartig (ed.), *Offenbarung—Schrift—Kirche*, Wuppertal-Bremen (1968). Journals and newsletters: *Bekenntnisbewegung "Kein anderes Evangelium"*; *Kirchliche Sammlung um Bibel und Bekenntnis*; *Lebendige Gemeinde* (newsletter of the *Ludwig-Hofacker-Vereinigung*); *Hörer-Echo* (Lutheran Radio Hour).

Translated by John Cumming

Arthur Macdonald Allchin

The Problem of "Orthodoxy"—the English-speaking Scene

THE problems which surround the question of orthodoxy in the Protestant Churches of the Anglo-Saxon language area are necessarily highly complex ones. None of the terms employed is easy to define. The geographical area in question is large and diffuse. The term "Protestant", apparently simple, has its own complications, since the Anglican Churches are sometimes reckoned among the denominations which go to make up English-speaking Protestantism, and sometimes not. As to the word "orthodoxy" the problems of defining it in this context are innumerable.

We can, however, introduce a certain measure of clarity into the discussion by saying that in this article the geographical area under review comprises the British Isles (primarily England and Scotland) and North America (i.e., the United States and Canada). There is theological activity in other parts of the English-speaking world (e.g., in Australasia or South Africa), but unquestionably the major centres of interest lie on either side of the North Atlantic.

I

Of the Churches involved, we include the Anglican, which provide the major, though not the only theological influence within the British Isles, and which are present in North America, though in the United States as a small minority. Among the various Churches with which we are concerned, there are very different traditions of theological thinking, very different attitudes towards the criteria of Christian orthodoxy, and very different understandings of the nature of the Church and its common confession of faith.

There are at least three major Church types to be distinguished: (1) the Confessional Protestant traditions (e.g., Lutheran in the United States, Reformed in Scotland), (2) the Free Church denominations, with their historical origins in England, but their main development in the United States (e.g., Methodist, Baptist and Congregationalist), and (3) the Anglican.

All these Churches recognize the supreme authority of Scripture in matters of faith. But the appeal to Scripture can mean different things in different places. The first group, though strongly influenced by the theological attitudes predominant in the English-speaking world, are of course closely linked with the main streams of continental European Protestantism, in which the confessional documents of the Reformation period have played a very large part in determining the bounds of Christian orthodoxy. In the second group, theological work has tended to develop in more individual and empirical ways, and there has often been a reluctance to bind the Churches to any fixed doctrinal standards. In the third case, that of the Anglicans, while reference to the sixteenth-century formulas has not been ruled out, the theological tradition has increasingly been influenced by the study of the first five centuries of Christian doctrine, and by the constant use of the ecumenical creeds in public worship. These facts have given Anglicans a somewhat different view of "orthodoxy" from that common among the majority of Protestants.[1]

But at least as important as these differences of attitude which stem from different confessional points of view, are the differences which result from the very different situations of the Churches on the two sides of the North Atlantic. On the European side, there

[1] It is worth noting that the Lambeth Conference of 1968 recommended that in future the clergy should either not be asked to assent to the 39 Articles at all, or that the assent should be contextualized in such a way as to make clear the relationship between the Articles and other more universal elements in the Church and tradition of faith and teaching, such as the ecumenical Creeds.

are old established national Churches in England and Scotland, facing the problems which arise when a national Church finds itself in an increasingly secularized society. In the case of England, there is a Church, which since the Reformation has attempted to combine conservation in structure with openness to new ideas, and a sense of corporate responsibility with a respect for individual freedom. In this, the history of the Church of England has been closely linked with that of a nation in which a certain capacity for change has been linked with an astonishing degree of traditionalism. This is necessarily a Church which feels the current theological crisis very vividly.

The dilemma is epitomized in the person of Dr J. A. T. Robinson, whose book *Honest to God* (London, 1963) was the symptom rather than the cause of the revolution which was already beginning to take place in the theology of the English-speaking world. Undoubtedly the fact that its author was a bishop was one of the reasons for the extraordinary impact which the book made on the general reading public. The teaching authority of the episcopate may not be very clearly defined in Anglicanism, but none the less a bishop is regarded (and not only by Anglicans) as being in some way the spokesman of the Church's common tradition and public confession of faith. It was partly because of the position which he held that the unfamiliar things which Bishop Robinson said caused such a sensation.

But although the traditionalism of Anglican thinking has been challenged severely by the current theological ferment, the element of continuity in Anglican Church life has acted as a counterbalance to the violence of change. Here again the position of Dr Robinson is interesting and typical. The fact that, although he is returning from diocesan to academic work, he continues to be very active in the life of the Church, and the fact that in his two more recent books, *The New Reformation* (London, 1965) and *Exploration into God* (London, 1967), he seems to be seeking to reappropriate elements of traditional Christianity which he had earlier neglected, suggest that within Anglicanism, and indeed within British theology as a whole, it is difficult to set radical and conservative too sharply against one another. The most typical theologians of this tradition refuse to be put down in one camp or the other.

In the *United States*, on the other hand, the situation is very different, much more complex and open and much more likely to go to extremes; but if it is distinctly confused, it is also distinctly hopeful. Here is a country with no established Church, with no one deeply rooted theological tradition, which, if it is secularized, is secularized in a very different way from Europe, and in which, in the years since the war, the Churches have known, at the material level at least, a considerable affluence and prosperity.

In so far as there is a typical American Christianity, it goes back to the particular type of Protestantism which the early settlers brought with them in the seventeenth century. In the first century of New England it was an intellectual tradition of a strict and systematic Calvinism,[2] combined with a fervent individual piety. During the eighteenth century it turned rapidly from a Reformed scholasticism into an English form of deism, which gave birth to American Unitarianism. It seems that in some measure American Protestantism has continued to oscillate between highly conservative authoritarian systems linked with strong religious feeling on the one side, which will provide very narrow definitions of Christian orthodoxy, and on the other, styles of theology and Christian living which tend to become little more than a Christian or religious colouring to the predominant movements of thought outside the Church and in which the concept of orthodoxy seems scarcely relevant. While it would certainly be impossible to describe the present situation in America solely in terms of the American past, it is helpful for those who approach it from outside to remember the very specific character of American religious history.

These preliminary considerations of the differentiating features within Anglo-Saxon Protestantism, which make it difficult to generalize on this subject, need to be supplemented by a brief survey of the development of theological thinking in the years since the last war, in which we can find much that is common to Britain and America alike. Only against this longer perspective can we begin to distinguish in the mass of theological writing

[2] On this subject see the brilliant studies of Perry G. E. Miller, *The New England Mind; the 17th Century* (New York, 1939), and *The New England Mind; From Colony to Province* (Cambridge, Mass., 1953).

which has marked the explosion of the last ten years, what is of lasting significance from what is merely ephemeral.

The crisis of the last decade would seem to be in part a reaction against, in part a development from, an earlier period whose dominant characteristics were consolidation and concentration on the specific nature of the Christian revelation and tradition, rather than an exploration of the possibility of relating the mystery of Christ to the developing problems and achievements of human society.

This earlier period, which extended down till about 1960, was the period of the so-called "neo-orthodoxy". It was marked, in all the Churches with which we are concerned, in the first place by a strong interest in biblical theology, a study and exposition of the biblical revelation, which while making use of the results of critical and historical scholarship was content to expound the Bible in its own terms. A fine and typical example of such work among the Anglicans could be seen in Alan Richardson, *An Introduction to the Theology of the New Testament* (London, 1958). An earlier but more speculative theologian, who in his lifetime had passed from philosophical to biblical theology, was L. S. Thornton, whose study *The Common Life in the Body of Christ* (London, 1941) was, as its title suggests, a study of the nature of the Church in the light of biblical imagery and ideas.[3] For this was also the period in which ecclesiology became a matter of central importance in the varying traditions of English-speaking Protestantism, a development stimulated by the formation of the World Council of Churches in 1948, in which all the Churches under review have participated. It was the time of what has been called ecclesiological ecumenism. Closely related to it was a concern for the doctrine of the sacraments, and in many places a rediscovery of the centrality of the liturgy. (Gregory's Dix's work, *The Shape of the Liturgy* [London, 1945], was of vital importance here.) For a variety of reasons, among them the all-pervasive influence of Karl Barth, felt indirectly in many places where his work was little studied, theology acquired a new confidence in itself, and a new

[3] In his later trilogy, under the general title *The Form of the Servant*, Thornton set out to study the specific nature of the forms of Christian revelation: *Revelation and the Modern World* (London, 1950), *The Dominion of Christ* (London, 1952) and *Christ and the Church* (London, 1956).

assurance that its work should begin from the Word of God given in Scripture, and mediated in tradition, rather than from the situation of contemporary man. But at the same time philosophical and fundamental theology suffered an eclipse.

II

The last decade has seen a sudden and dramatic change in this situation. The reasons for the revolution are many. In part doubtless it comes from a different world situation, which if it is still full of menace can yet give rise to an optimism about the future of mankind which would have seemed naïve in the years immediately after the war. In part it is due to the pressures of the social and technological revolutions which are forcing theologians to rethink their understanding of man and society, and which are showing that however necessary a "return to the sources" may be for Christian theology, it can never involve a return to an earlier phase of Christian culture, to a Christendom which has for ever departed. But there has also been a kind of explosion within theology itself, which has made many of the exponents of the methods of biblical theology face different questions, and confront new areas both of contemporary human experience, and of the Church's historical tradition.

Undoubtedly a further vital element within this revolution has been the parallel development within Roman Catholic thinking since the Council. The mood of openness towards the world, and the desire to read the signs of the times, which characterized the inspiration of Pope John, have been of decisive influence on the development of Christian thinking outside, no less than inside the Roman Catholic Church.

In speaking of an explosion or revolution in the theological world one is not merely using terms of rhetoric. Something has changed radically and rapidly. There is an unprecedented freedom of theological discussion, and a manifest desire to return to the most fundamental theological questions about the being and nature of God, his relationship to mankind and creation. As if by an inherent dynamism, the ecumenical dialogue of the forties and fifties, which tended to concentrate on the secondary though important questions of sacraments and Church order, has been taken back to the basic questions of the being of God and revelation in Christ.

At the same time a new public for theology seems to have come into existence; there is a new interest in the discussion of theological matters in often unexpected places. The effects of this development are various. On the one side is a "newspaper theology" which requires the sensational writing up of extreme positions, and frequent changes in theological fashion—perhaps every two years or so. On the other side the growth of paperback book publishing and the extremely large sales of some popular but serious theological works have encouraged many theologians to try to write in a more accessible and immediately relevant way, so as to reach a larger and less specialized public. It seems as if a new class of reader is growing, largely lay and sometimes only loosely affiliated to the Churches. In this situation tensions appear in all the Churches between the new questioning mood of a lay theology deeply concerned with secular realities, and older and more traditional forms of Christian thinking and feeling.

In this situation of extreme fluidity, it becomes difficult to know what is "orthodox" and what is not, and most theologians are very reluctant to make quick decisions. It seems as though in the varying new schools of thought, tendencies which are genuinely out of harmony with the Christian tradition understood in its fullness lie side by side with others, which are only apparently at odds with "orthodoxy" or which are in revolt against "orthodoxies" of a local or more recent kind. If we examine typical areas where theology is coming into closer contact with contemporary schools of philosophy, we can perhaps see examples of this fact. In America, for instance, there is a renewed movement to make use of the categories of "process philosophy" associated with the work of Charles Hartshorne, in order to elucidate the Christian mystery.[4] Here there is a desire to see the evolutionary process in terms of the activity of God, which at times seems to lead to seeing God simply as the totality of the process, at other times to seeing him at the heart of the process, but himself greater than it.

[4] For a good, brief account of this development see Norman Pittenger, *God in Process* (London, 1967). See also J. A. Martin, *The New Dialogue between Philosophy and Theology* (New York, 1966). The parallels with the thought of Teilhard de Chardin are sometimes striking here.

Again in England there have been developments in theological thinking intended to bring theology into closer contact with the linguistic philosophy which has been dominant in the British Isles for thirty years or more. In some of its exponents this move seems to lead towards remarkable restatements of the Christian position, in others towards a complete acceptance of the presuppositions as well as the methods of the current philosophy.[5]

In the same way the whole movement towards a theology of the secular, whether in its more personalist form in a writer like Ronald Gregor Smith, *Secular Christianity* (London, 1966), or in its more social and political version in the work of Harvey Cox, *The Secular City* (New York, 1965), looks towards the discovery of God in and through this world. But the question remains as to whether or not it looks for God exclusively in this way. In sharp contrast with this tendency to see the activity of God primarily in the development of the Western secular world is the new willingness of some theologians to look for signs of the divine activity in the other religious traditions of mankind. Notable re-interpretations of the significance of Islam, from a Christian point of view, have come from Kenneth Cragg, for instance, and this writer has more recently extended his attention to other of the great religions.[6] Similarly in John Macquarrie, *Principles of Christian Theology* (New York, 1966), there is a valuable and original discussion of "Religion and Religions" (*op. cit.*, pp. 134–58). But here again there is a tension between more inclusive ways of interpreting the uniqueness of Christianity, and explorations which deny this uniqueness altogether.

Perhaps of all the theological movements of this period, it has been the "Death of God" controversy which has gained the greatest publicity. But beneath the slogans very different theologies have been concealed, in the work for instance of Thomas Altizer, *The Gospel of Christian Atheism* (Philadelphia, 1966), or William Hamilton, *The New Essence of Christianity* (New

[5] For this see Ian T. Ramsey, *Religious Language* (London, 1957), and *Models and Mystery* (London, 1964).

[6] Kenneth Cragg, *The Call of the Minaret* (New York, 1956), *The Dome and the Rock* (London, 1964). *Christianity in World Perspective* (London, 1963), *The Privilege of Man* (London, 1965).

York, 1961).[7] Nietzsche's startling and prophetic words have meant and mean many things to many people; that God has always been dead, that he died at a particular moment, that some image of him has collapsed, that some era of religious feeling and understanding has come to an end. It is evident that some interpretations of the phrase will be less "orthodox" than others. But it will take time and wisdom to discern the real significance of all that is being said.

In all these and many other areas it is impossible to know how the movements of thought will develop and change. One brief but notable attempt at an assessment of the situation has been made by Dr A. M. Ramsey in his *God, Christ and the World; a Study in Contemporary Theology* (London, 1969). Another, and much larger-scale assessment, also from an Anglican point of view, emerges from the work of John Macquarrie, who has come to be recognized as one of the leading spokesmen of a position which refuses the dichotomy of radical and conservative.[8] As a leading authority on the thought of Martin Heidegger in the English-speaking world, and as one who has been deeply influenced by the work of Rudolf Bultmann, Macquarrie could hardly be considered a purely conservative theologian. Yet at the same time he insists strongly on the givenness and continuity of the Christian life and tradition, in which and for which the theologian must work. "To deny fundamental doctrines, like that of the Trinity; to reject the Creeds; to set aside the beliefs of the early councils of the still undivided Church—these may be actions to which individuals are impelled by their own thinking on these matters, but they cannot take place in Christian theology, for they amount to a rejection of the history and therefore of the continuing identity of the community within which Christian theologizing takes place."[9]

[7] T. W. Ogletree, *The Death of God Controversy* (London, 1966), provides a brief account.

[8] Cf. *Twentieth-century Religious Thought* (London, 1963), *Principles of Christian Theology* (New York, 1966) and *God-Talk* (London, 1967).

[9] *Principles of Christian Theology*, p. 11. A different approach to the problems of philosophy and theology, but equally unclassifiable in terms of "conservatism" or "radicalism" is to be found in Donald MacKinnon, *Borderlands of Theology* (London, 1969). D. L. Edwards in *Religion and Change* (London, 1969) provides a far-reaching survey of the whole field.

Meanwhile it has become evident that all the barriers are down between theologians of the different Christian traditions, and this is one of the most important developments of the last ten years. The sense that we all face a common situation and are searching together for new ways in which to live and express the mystery of Christ is overwhelmingly strong. The days of a cautious or confessional ecumenism are past, as also are those of any partial "orthodoxy". To find what "orthodoxy" really is will be a common task for all the Churches. This new situation makes it more necessary than ever that theological contacts should be drawn closer between thinkers of different traditions and different language areas. In the last decade the translation of much from German Catholic writing (above all, of course, Karl Rahner) has introduced a new element into the Anglo-Saxon theological debate. In the United States the dialogue has extended beyond the purely Christian world and includes an active Jewish participation. The insistence of a writer like Emil Fackenheim on the transcendence of God has provided a valuable counterbalance to fashionable tendencies in theology, too easily accepted.[10]

The period of the 1960s has been a hectic one, and we need the discovery of a new sense of proportion. We need perhaps a more living understanding that the Christian tradition is something older than the Reformation, older than Western Scholasticism. Did the Fathers of the Church really hellenize the gospel, or were they true to its essential message? What does the apophatic tradition of patristic theology have to say to our controversy over the death of God? Suggestions of this kind may be found in the work of D. E. Jenkins, *A Guide to the Debate about God* (London, 1965), and *The Glory of Man* (London, 1967). H. W. Richardson, in a book which has been too little recognized, *Toward an American Theology* (New York, 1967), draws together a deep knowledge of the present changes in human society and life, with a feeling for the value and significance of many areas of the Christian tradition. In his discussion of the work and person of the Holy Spirit, there is an attempt to

[10] Emil Fackenheim, *The Quest for Past and Future* (Bloomington, Indiana, 1969).

re-think ancient and neglected themes from the earlier Christian tradition, in the light of insights which have come from the more recent experience of Free Church Christianity. Is it perhaps here, in a renewed doctrine of the personal presence of the Holy Spirit in the Church and in each person, that we have the clue to rediscovering orthodoxy, not as an externally imposed pattern but as a true and living glorification of the generosity of God?

PART III
DOCUMENTATION
CONCILIUM

Concilium General Secretariat

The Creed in the Melting Pot

THE opening session of Vatican II was marred by an apparently small incident concerning the official confession of faith. According to canon law, an important gathering of the Church about "faith and morals" such as an ecumenical council should be opened with a solemn confession of the Church's faith. For this occasion the organizers had planned to use a simplified version of the creed commonly recited at such solemn functions.[1] In actual fact, the creed of the Council of Trent was chosen. Guests from other, particularly Protestant, Churches were somewhat astonished that this particular creed, larded with theological controversy, was used at the opening of a Council that described itself explicitly as ecumenical.

It is curious that the new version of the creed, which contained quotations from Pius XII's encyclical *Humani Generis*, was never again mentioned in the subsequent sessions of the Council. In contrast with previous Councils, Vatican II, which was officially described as a pastoral[2] Council, did not deal with the question of

[1] O. Karrer, "Das Bekenntnis der Bischöfe", in J. C. Hampe, *Die Autorität der Freiheit*, I (Munich, 1967), p. 62 and n. 2; for historical background and literature, see K. Lehmann, "Bedarf das Glaubensbekenntnis einer Neufassung?", in *Veraltetes Glaubensbekenntnis?* (Regensburg, 1968), pp. 125–86, esp. n. 140 and n. 29.

[2] The adjective "pastoral" proved ambiguous in practice: many problems were disposed of by asserting that this was a "pastoral" and not a "doctrinal" Council. It is of the essence of an ecumenical council that it is integral, cf. M. D. Chenu, "La rénovation de la théologie morale", in *Vie Spir.* (suppl.), 90 (Sept. 1969), p. 289.

possible additions to the official creed, and the Fathers went home before a new formulation of the creed had been announced. In view of the statements about the bishops' collegiality with the Pope, nobody expected the publication of an official creed behind the back of the episcopal college. There was therefore great surprise when Pope Paul published his authoritative creed at the conclusion of the Year of Faith on 30 June 1968, which coincided with the solemn opening of the fourth general assembly of the World Council of Churches in Uppsala.[3] For many Christians, both inside and outside the Catholic communion, this solemn confession composed by the Pope came as an answer to their demand for greater certainty about what was still to be believed today, while for others it sharpened a conflict which, after an incubation period of half a century, threatened to break out among the faithful.[4] This controversy about a new formulation of the creed is far from settled. It is felt acutely among the new generation of Christians whose problems are the proper concern of a periodical such as *Concilium* which aims at pursuing the theological and pastoral inspiration of Vatican II. This Documentation hopes to provide the background to the problem as well as a systematic survey.

It is perhaps useful, particularly in connection with the article by Brekelmans, to start with some general information about the existence and function of the creed in Judaism and some non-Christian religions lest the reader should have the impression that the creed is something peculiar to Christians. We shall then proceed to sketch the historical development of the apostolic and other creeds. This will be followed by a survey of the attempts made to compose a creed that is viable and acceptable to our age

[3] L. Visscher 't Hooft, *Kommentar zu der Ansprache des Papstes vom 30. Juni 1968* (Uppsala Release n. UP-13).

[4] W. Kasper, *Dogma unter dem Wort Gottes* (Mainz, 1965), p. 52. This incubation process was stimulated in the last century by the authorities' constant fear that modernism would rear its fearful head again. Groups like *Confrontatie* always nervously describe any attempt at renewal as "neo-modernism" or with phrases like "on nous change la foi" (they are changing our faith). R. Aubert, "Alfred Loisy, der 'Vater des Modernismus'", in *Orientierung*, 32 (22 Nov. 1968), pp. 246–9; art. "Modernism", in *Sacramentum Mundi*, IV (London and New York), pp. 99 ff.

and culture, the drafting of what Rahner has called a "brief formula" (*Kurzformel*), after Luther.[5]

1. *Do only Christians have a Creed?*

Now that we are better informed about other religions, it is no longer possible today to assert without further qualification that a confession of faith in the form of a handy creed is the exclusive preserve of Christian Churches. P. Brunner[6] has pointed out that all religions founded on a revelation know of a creed, even the religions of Iran, Mohammedanism[7] and Hinayana Buddhism.[8] As became clear at last year's World Assembly of mainly intellectual Mohammedans in Kuala Lumpur, there is even a demand for a new confession of faith in Mohammedanism.

It has often been asserted, both by those who think it an advantage and by those who think it a failing, that Christianity is distinguished from all other religions by the fact that it has in the creed a well-defined and easily intelligible description of the main points of its teaching. Recent studies, however, have shown that the presence or absence of such a key formula for the believer's faith and practice of this faith does not depend on the doctrinal or non-doctrinal character of a particular religion but rather on the growth of a confessing community, the members of which find their identity in such a creed. Religions of peoples as such, for instance, do not have a creed because there the religious conviction is intertwined with the popular awareness of being a

[5] K. Lehmann, *loc. cit.*, p. 173, refers to three small books which Luther published in 1520 under a common title: *Eine kurze Form der 10 Gebote, Eine kurze Form des Glaubens* and *Eine kurze Form des Vaterunsers*, VII (Weimar edn.), pp. 204–29. H. Dörries, *Das Bekenntnis in der Geschichte der Kirche* (2nd edn., Göttingen, 1959), pp. 82 f., mentions other such short formulas composed by B. Pascal, Spener, Zinzendorf, etc.

[6] "Wesen und Funktion von Glaubenbekenntnissen", in *Veraltetes Glaubensbekenntnis* (Regensburg, 1968), pp. 7–11, and the bibliography indicated there.

[7] A. J. Wensinck, *The Muslim Creed. Its Genesis and Historical Development* (London, 1965), pp. 3, 19, 102 and 270; for the earliest conflict between Christian and Mohammedan creeds in the East, cf. A. J. Visser, "De vroeg-christelijke sekten", in *Spiegel Historiael*, 4 and 5 (May 1969), pp. 260–5.

[8] Art. "Bekenntnis", in *Die Religion in Geschichte u. Gegenwart*, I (Tübingen, 1957), cc. 988–91 ("Religionsgeschichtlich", by G. Mensching, and "Im Alten Testament und im Judentum", by C. Westermann).

people or a nation. Thus Miguel de Unamuno once said that it is impossible for a Spaniard to be heterodox because his Christianity coincides with his national self-awareness. On the other hand, religions that claim to be universal and have a missionary character all have a creed. Such a briefly formulated doxological creed indicates that, in religions of this type, the faith originates in "hearing", in a message, a living word that communicates something new and helps the believer and his fellow believers to identify themselves. In this sense G. van der Leeuw[9] maintains that it is characteristic of each creed to refer back to the spoken word and then to express itself via the spoken word in so far as the recitation of the creed in public worship indicates precisely what makes this group a community and ensures the identity of this believing community.

At first sight Judaism does not seem to fit in with this description of the creed. There the belonging to one people and belief seem to cover each other completely. Many recent authors agree with von Rad[10] that this is not the case.

Israel has always experienced a tension between its nationalism and its belief, and Israel, too, has its creed through which the Jew identifies himself as a believer. Not only the Shema Yizrael of Deuteronomy (Hear Israel, I am your God), often considered the only summary indication of a creed in Israel, but also the thanksgiving for definite and historical saving deeds of "Yahweh our God" increasingly acquired the quality of an explicit creed.

A certain rationalization of these narrative and doxological creeds can be found in the so-called *thirteen rules* in which the most important thinker of medieval Jewry, Moses Maimonides, summed up the essence of Judaism and which lives on in Jewish worship as Jigdal in a poetic form.[11] A creed, used in the liturgical service, was also discovered in the Qumran community.[12]

[9] G. van der Leeuw, *Phänomenologie der Religion* (2nd edn., 1956), p. 503.

[10] G. von Rad, *Das fünfte Buch Mose* (Göttingen, 1964), p. 113. W. Molinski, in the collection, *Die viele Wege zum Heil—Heilsanspruch und Heilsbedeutung nichtchristlicher Religionen* (Munich, 1969), still clings to the antiquated idea that Christianity alone has a definite creed.

[11] K. Hruby, "Eléments de spiritualité juive", in *La mystique et les mystiques* (Bruges/Paris, 1965), pp. 159 f. and bibliogr., pp. 255–6.

[12] H. Bardtke, "Das Ich des Meisters in den Hodajoth von Qumran", in *Wissenschaftliche Zeitschrift Leipzig*, 6 (1956–57), pp. 93–104.

These brief indications may suffice to show that the creed of the early Church was no novelty but a harmonious continuation of a tradition of credal formulas in Judaism. In all probability the Christian converts from Judaism used the Shema Yizrael as a creed when they gathered in the temple, with the addition that the promises of Yahweh were fulfilled in Jesus.

All these creeds show a common feature: they help the believer to express his belief (*medium fidei*) in common prayer and so to recognize his fellow believers and his own identity.[13] Originally the emphasis did not fall on the doctrinal, and certainly not on the juridical, aspect of the creed. The creed was not held as the object of the act of faith but pointed to the reality towards which this act of faith was directed, namely, the God who could be identified by his deeds.

2. *The Historical Development of the Creeds*

It would be unhistorical to try to interpret the presence in the history of the Church of creeds and summaries of religious teaching which differ in their formulation as a definitive and unchangeable original creed which gave birth to a whole generation of formulas, all derived from this single one. The history of the early Church rather suggests the spontaneous emergence of many creeds in the various local Churches where one group would show features indicating a Jewish milieu while some other group would show features belonging to the Greco-Roman civilization of the time.

While in Syrian churches we see a group of creeds with seven articles, the region dominated by the Greco-Roman civilization have variations of the creed in twelve articles which historically developed into the so-called Apostles' creed. In the West, Milan, Turin, Ravenna, Florence, Toledo, the Churches of Africa, and, at the time of Charlemagne, Gaul, had their own creeds.[14] Yet, a believer coming from Jerusalem was recognized in Ravenna as

[13] J. Ratzinger, *Einführung in das Christentum*, p. 66, says that this symbol of two pieces that fit together was already used in antiquity to recognize a messenger or a guest, a kind of passport with which to establish someone's identity.

[14] For the texts of the various creeds, see A. Hahn, *Bibliothek der Symbole und Glaubensregeln der alten Kirche* (with an appendix by A. von Harnack (3rd edn., Breslau, 1897); J. N. D. Kelly, *Early Christian Creeds*

a true Christian and a son of the new Israel. The creeds were not opposed to each other but were harmonious variations on one and the same theme, the worshipping recognition of God's deeds of salvation in Jesus of Nazareth.

This peaceful co-existence of different creeds is easy to understand when we remember the original function of the creed: to be a *medium fidei*, a means by which people confessed their common faith in prayer. Where the creed later became also the norm of faith (*norma fidei*) and, after the early apologists and the beginnings of various kinds of theology, also a doctrinal norm (*norma doctrinae*), and finally the test of orthodoxy to be applied to Christians who sought their salvation in other directions (*norma orthodoxiae*), the multiplicity of creeds became a threat to unity.

The Eastern, but later on also the Western, Emperors turned the creed into a political instrument in order to establish or restore the unity of the empire. It then became a kind of imperial charter, or part of it. History indeed shows that attempts to establish centralization in Church and Empire went hand in hand with the development of a uniform creed. In spite of the political influence of the Emperors on the creeds of various councils (the most peculiar is probably that of Ephesus, summoned by Theodosius in 431) and the incorporation of the creed in the *Codex Justinianus*,[15] several different creeds continued to exist side by side in the East. In the West the Apostles' creed of the third century, later called the Roman creed, became more and more the norm, not only for the faith, but also for political purposes, something Charlemagne encouraged only too willingly. The legend that the Apostles' creed with its twelve articles was composed by the Apostles themselves, one article each, arose only in the sixth century.

As the function of the creed became more juridical and doctrinal, the gaps in the doctrine showed up more clearly. The Apostles' creed does not contain all that belongs to the official

---

(2nd edn., London, 1960), and for the Syrian Church, R. H. Connolly, "The Early Syriac Creeds", in *Zeitschr. f. n.t. Wiss. und die Kunde der älteren Kirche*, 7 (1906), pp. 202–23.

[15] A. Ehrhardt, art. "Justinian I", in *Rel. in Gesch. u. Gegenw.*, III (3rd edn., 1959), cc. 1076–7; A. J. Visser, *loc. cit.*, and W. Maurer, "Bekenntnis" (rechtlich), in *Rel. in Gesch. u. Gegenw.*, I (3rd edn.), c. 1003.

teaching. The development of dogma began to take over the function of the creed, and the growth of the creed was stunted.

This historical split between the Apostles' creed and dogmatic teaching created a difficulty for the Reformers from the beginning. The doctrine of justification, at the very heart of the Reformation, is not mentioned in the Apostles' creed. Luther knew quite well that the Apostles' creed could also be understood with the confession of the forgiveness of sins as its central theme, and that there was no need to incorporate his historically conditioned approach to justification explicitly in the Apostles' creed. He said several times that he did not wish to argue about the creed and its content: "This is my Bible. . . . I have no intention of going beyond."[16] For him—and this is important for the function of the creed—the creed is an authoritative text which he compares to the Our Father and which he advises people to recite as a prayer. Here he is at one with the tradition of the doxological function of the creed.[17] One might even say that he re-discovered the confessional and doxological function of the creed and reinforced it with the composition of hymns to give expression to the faith. The doctrinal aspects were left to such rules of faith as the Confession of Augsburg, etc., which could not be used in the liturgical service because of their length.

The creed of the Council of Trent has passages which are clearly confessional and others that are plainly doctrinal. The unfortunate result of this mixing of the confessional with the doctrinal is that interpretations become items to be believed, and so the doctrinal interpretation and expansion becomes an object of faith. This intellectualizing of the creed and the introduction of theological terminology spoiled the linguistic play of the original confession and ruined the peaceful co-existence of creeds in various local Churches.

The result was that one creed was meant to oppose another. The object of the confession was no longer the identity of the living God but the different way of confessing on controversial grounds. The creeds then no longer served the building of the community but became divisive factors (schism). The prohibition

[16] Cf. *WA*, 37, 55.

[17] Cf. *Die Bekenntnisschriften der ev-luth. Kirche* (3rd edn., Göttingen, 1956), pp. 521 f.

of Trent and the Roman catechism against using any other forms of confession than those employing the terminology of the Council of Trent and the Counter-Reformation signed the death warrant of a legitimate pluralism of creeds and consequently of a legitimate pluralism of catechisms. The uniform catechism began to look like a means of indoctrination. This process also paralysed the growth of the language of faith. The creativity of the believer who makes up his own language in the confession, and so brings a constant freshness to all talk about salvation, is blocked. This can already be seen in the changing terminology in the creeds: instead of the *"credo"* (*ik geloof*) of the Apostles' creed, the creed of Nicaea and still in the original version of that of Constantinople, we now have a *"docemus confiteri"* (we teach that the following must be confessed, in the sense of showing forth).

The creed is no longer a sign of recognition but a test-case of the trustworthiness (we might say, security) of an in-group over against those outside. The universal character of the creed, then, has virtually evaporated, something that was painfully experienced by the missionaries of various Churches and led to the Faith and Order movement.

If in the tenth and eleventh centuries the creed may be said to suffer from cramp, after 1568 this turned into a lasting paralysis. And so, in our desire for a new formulation of the creed today we are faced with the question of whether this historical paralysis can be cured and how. In matters of faith, too, creativity is not something that can be brought about by order.[18]

It might be thought that this cramp-situation was caused by the historicity of the permanently normative Apostles' creed. This does not seem to be the case. The historical untenability of the legend about the origin of the Apostles' creed was admitted soon enough, and yet, the authority of this creed remained as it was.[19]

Without entering into detail about what caused this growing rigidity we may say that the two main causes were a too narrow

[18] Cf. the special issue of *Parole et Mission* (15 Oct. 1969), n. 47, "Malaises autour de la confession de foi", and particularly O. Costa de Beauregard, "Ma foi chrétienne en 1970".

[19] Cf. H. Dörries, *op. cit.* In Germany there was even a so-called "Apostolikumstreit", cf. "Apostolikum II", in *Rel. in Gesch. u. Gegenw.*, 1 (3rd edn.), by G. Hoffmann.

concept of the unity of faith and a too static and ontological concept of the identity of this faith with that of "our fathers in the faith". Then the juridical insistence on the once established formula is taken as a guarantee for the unity and continuity of the faith. But the history of the last four centuries shows that, in actual fact, this kills the creativity of the faith.

This lack of creativity is still underlined by the fact that the confession of the creed becomes a secondary factor in the prayer of the Church. It is not really exaggerating to say that the impasse which now besets the creed can be compared with that which is bedevilling the saying of the office with the breviary. The multiplicity of offices and prayers was reduced by Trent, and the reason was stated explicitly to be "to eliminate variety in prayer" (*ad tollendam varietatem orationis*). The result was that creativity in this field of prayer also did not stand a chance.

Something similar happened when the uniformity of the creed was carried through. The exploitation of the doctrinal and dogmatic function of the creed pushed its liturgical and doxological function into the background.[20] For the same reasons the renewal of the liturgy and the introduction of the vernacular made the sad state of the creed, long covered up by the use of Latin, more acute. And this holds not only for the Catholic Church, but, up to a point, also for the Protestant Churches.[21]

The Protestant Churches were sooner aware of this evil situation. When Söderblom made his first attempts at setting up a World Council of Churches, an effort was made to bring the Protestant Churches, from extreme orthodox to extreme liberal, with their differences in doctrines and confession, together by means of a kind of mini-creed. This effort which aimed at establishing a

[20] For the function of the creed, see H. Dombois (canon lawyer of the Ev. Ch.), who in his *Das Recht der Gnade* (2nd edn., Witten, 1969), pp. 691 f., says that this connection of the creed with the liturgy is necessary in order to prevent a distortion of both the one and the other. W. Kasper, *op. cit.*, pp. 32 f., stresses the connection between liturgy and dogma in the Eastern Church.

[21] Protestant student groups, for instance, found it necessary to create new creeds for their modern services, as happened in Bonn, but this holds also for other youth services. Cf. H. Keller, "Bekenntnisbildung in der Gegenwart", in *Bekenntnis in Bewegung* (Göttingen, 1969), pp. 167 f.

doctrinal minimum by means of reduction came to a poor end.[22] When one compares the laborious struggle at the beginning of the World Council to achieve a minimum of universally accepted teaching with the definitive text of Uppsala on "our common confession"[23] one is struck by the fact that the doctrinal character of the confession is not referred to but only the practical consequences. These are summed up in four basic features: a confession must have some influence in the world (revolutionary character); it must be the result of corporate action (it must not come from one person or one Church but from the "World Confessional Families"[24]); it must always have the character of a response, i.e., one can only confess against the background of God confessing himself to mankind, God's own confession, and the history through which God confesses himself to mankind can no longer be unmade; finally, such a confession can never again be a confession in opposition to the world as if it were something that does not belong to the world: it must be conditioned and required by the world.

At first sight this seems to tend towards a kind of Christian pragmatism or a sociologized Christianity, as if it does not matter what people confess as long as they confess in a way which has some effect on the world. But this is only apparently so. The World Council is also convinced that the matter of confession is not a matter of indifference. What it stresses is that what is confessed cannot be a mere repetition of what was said in the past since this is a language which is no longer common property and therefore is in danger of not being understood at all.

This question of language really broaches a fundamental problem.[25] In a penetrating analysis Theunis has shown that Europe

[22] For the history of the creed of the World Council see R. Bultmann, "Das christologische Bekenntnis des ökumenischen Rates", in *Glauben und Verstehen*, II (3rd edn., Tübingen, 1961), pp. 246–61, and W. Theurer, *Die trinitarische Basis des ökumenischen Rates der Kirchen* (Bergen-Enkheim, 1967).

[23] Cf. the address given by R. Bertram, "Unser gemeinsames Bekenntnis und seine Konsequenzen für unsere Zeit", in *Reden* (n. 4), Ökum. Rat der Kirchen, 4, Vollversammlung (Uppsala, July 1968).

[24] The importance of the World Confessional Families is emphasized in the *Auschuss-Dokument*, I, *Glaube und Kirchenverfassung* of the WCC (Uppsala, July 1968), pp. 9–18.

[25] No detailed analysis is possible here but an important contribution can

is on this point far behind America and that in Western Europe this aspect of Christian language has practically not been studied at all.[26] He says that the ability to speak is infected by anachronism and a kind of disease, but shows that this worn-out religious language is not dead because the evangelical message has not yet been enunciated in world-speech (*Weltgespräch*). Less encouraging still, Robinson suggested that it would be better to keep silent about some aspects of the confession for the time being.[27] This is impossible if we want to do this throughout the whole of Christendom. There is belief where people speak as believers. There is only confession in so far as people confess, however difficult the act of confession may have become today. An absolute silence about belief is impossible and would be a betrayal of the revelatory character of Christianity.

Any consideration of a possible new creed must imply the realization of the fundamental difficulties that arise from religious language, otherwise the attempt will simply become an amateurish manipulation of the situation by adjustment.[28] One should remember that language is something given. Man does not create language, and certainly not the language of confession. He is bound to the language in which twenty centuries of Christianity have confessed. He finds this language. This language also carries a reality which he does not control, and which forces him to confess more in that language than only his belief. He also confesses a body of culture with, on the fringe, some unbelief and superstition. This does not matter as long as he does not become a slave to it.

Linguistic analysis rightly draws our attention to the fact that

---

be expected from linguistic analysis in the future, also for the confessional language of Christians. I refer here to J. L. Austin, *Philosophical Papers* (Oxford, 1961); D. D. Evans, *The Logic of Self-Involvement*: A philosophical study of everyday language with special reference to the Christian use of language about God as Creator (London, 1963), and the art. by J. A. Ladrière, "Langage auto-implicatif et langage biblique selon Evans", in *Tijdschr. v. Filosofie*, 28 (1966), 3, pp. 441–94.

[26] F. Theunis, "Zur Sprache des Glaubens", in *Weltgespräch*, 7, with the heading "Sprache und Wahrheit, Zweite Folge" (1969), pp. 16–31.

[27] J. A. T. Robinson, *The New Reformation* (London, SCM Press); cf. J. Sperna Weiland, *Oriëntatie* (Baarn, 1966), pp. 103 f.

[28] *Ibid.*

any formulated statement indeed says and reveals something but at the same time hides a great deal. One might think that this drawback can be avoided by clinging faithfully to a once established formula.[29] But then we forget that language, too, is subject to wear-and-tear and must constantly be renewed to re-discover its power to say something meaningful.[30] The question is whether this is possible at this moment. In any case, it is striking that the demand for a new formulation of the creed is most powerfully voiced in those countries where linguistic analysis and structuralism are studied most, in the English-speaking countries, in Germany and in France.[31] Whether this is leading to some definite results we shall see in the last part of this documentation.

For these historical reasons it is almost obvious that the creed which the Pope published on 30 June 1968 as the creed of the People of God was not received with universal enthusiasm. There were few official reactions.[32] This may be because, one month after this creed, *Humanae Vitae* appeared and diverted attention from this problem which is urgent but has no immediate appeal, apart from the fact that most people are only too anxious to steer clear of it.

It is already commonplace to say that the faith has lost the quality of being self-evident. This implies that this faith cannot any longer convey its message all by itself either. The Pope's creed still presupposes that this faith is self-evident. As Congar

[29] W. Huster, *Sinnvolles Glaubensbekenntnis heute*. Laiengedanken zu theologischen Fragen der Gegenwart (Experiment Christentum 4) (Munich, 1969) is not very helpful.

[30] Cf. S. Ijsseling, "Gezag en vrijheid" (with Eng. summary), in *Tijdschr. v. Theol.*, 9 (1969), pp. 249–68.

[31] Y. Congar, K. Rahner and E. Schillebeeckx already mentioned the need for a brief formula of faith in an interview reported in *Inf. cath. intern.*, 290 (15 June 1967), pp. 16–19.

[32] J. Daniélou, "La profession de foi de Paul VI", in *Etudes* (Nov. 1968), pp. 599–607; L. M. Armendariz, "Los enunciados de la fe" (Cristianismo para hoy), in *Razón y Fe* 178, 846/7 (July/Aug. 1968), pp. 23–40; G. Card. Garrone, *La profession de foi de Paul VI*. Introduction (Coll. Pour le Peuple de Dieu, 1, Paris, 1969). As far as we know, the most complete commentary is that by C. Pozo, *El Credo del Pueblo de Dios*. Commentario teológico a la Profesión de S.S. Pablo VI (Madrid, BAC, 1968). 240 pp.

remarked, it is a retrospective creed.[33] It wants to recall the rich past of the faith, still present in the Church. For reasons one can understand, the Pope did not take the risk of publishing a prospective creed. As a sign of witness and an attempt to rouse personal zeal this creed has some value, but it would have been of greater value if this creed had been composed in co-operation with the college of bishops so that it would stress the subject of this confession, the community of believers, with greater clarity for our time. One is struck by the fact that the Pope chose formulas from practically every century of Christianity, and doctrinal rather than kerygmatic ones. This brings out still more clearly the static and historical aspect of this creed. Some authors have pointed out that this papal creed embodied all the objections to the kerygmatic formulation of the New Dutch Catechism, which managed to create religious language that can be understood today.[34] It is also clear that this creed is an attack on an anti-metaphysical tendency in the kerygmatic formulation and underlines the ontological reality of the truths expressed in the articles of faith.[35]

3. *Description and Situation of the Present Problem*

The historicity of the creed, the opinions about the nature of the Church's unity, the present difficulties which beset religious language within the general linguistic crisis, the difficulties inherent in this matter of confessing itself, created by a Christendom that has lost its self-evidence and has had to yield its social privilege to other movements—all this has brought to the fore, in a most distressing fashion, the problem of the reformulation of the creed, which for so long was kept under the table. The problem has become still more acute because it has given rise to a polarization which affects both Catholics and non-Catholics. On the one hand, we have those who want to maintain the doctrinal character of the old creed at all costs and use it as a way of excluding

[33] Y. Congar discussed the Pope's creed in *Au milieu des orages. L'Eglise affronte aujourd'hui son avenir* (Paris, 1969), pp. 58–65.

[34] Cf. G. Zizola, "Loin de toute passion. Pour le changement et la nouveauté", in *Inf. cath. intern.*, 316 (15 July 1968), pp. 9–11.

[35] Cf. the critical review "Problemberichte zum Zeitgeschehen. Bemühungen um eine 'Kurzformel' des Glaubens", in *Herderkorrespondenz*, 23, 1 (Jan. 1969), pp. 37 f.

other Christians. This tendency sees the function of the creed only as constituting the boundary of the institutional Church, and we find examples of it within the Catholic Church in such movements as the *Bewegung für Papst und Katholizismus, l'Homme nouveau, Confrontatie.* Among Protestants we have here *Kein anderes Evangelium, Bekennende Christen.*[36] These movements emphasize the stability of the creed's doctrinal content as eternal truths, the clear delimitation of the Church with regard to the world, and of the Church of the teachers over against the Church of the taught.

The other tendency emphasizes the function of the creed for the practice of the faith, is less interested in the content than in the act of faith, tries to break down the barriers between Church and world, the *magisterium* and the faithful. Extreme examples of this tendency can be found in such movements as the *Underground Churches, Kritischer Katholizismus* and *Tegenspraak.*[37] Neither of these two tendencies is peculiar to Catholicism but runs right across all the Churches, and can also be observed in such world-wide ideologies as Marxism. They point to the new level of spiritual awareness, the dawn of a new phase in culture where Christianity will have to play a different part, and they point, perhaps subconsciously, to the fear of the trials to which any belief is now exposed because of the progress of the sciences.

Karl Jaspers once said that the Churches with their mutually opposing confessions are no longer able to serve mankind on its way towards unification.[38] As an alternative he suggests that a philosophical faith (*filosophische Glaube*) should take over the function of the religions based on revelation.[39] One philosophy is, however, as much a utopia as one belief. Rahner, supported by

[36] Cf. the Bulletins by W. Dietzfelbinger and A. M. Allchin in this issue. See also U. Schwarz, "Wer ist katholisch? Anmerkungenzu einer Bewegung für Papst und Kirche", in *Publik*, 2 (25 June 1969), p. 24.

[37] "Kritischer Katholizismus" is the name of a group built up round the periodical with the same name in Germany. They also published a book under the same title (Frankfurt, 1968). A similar group with the name of "Kollektief" has recently begun to publish a periodical, *Tegenspraak* (Hilversum).

[38] K. Jaspers, *Philosophische Glaube* (1948).

[39] Similar positions were already held in the nineteenth century and the beginning of the twentieth by thinkers like H. Spencer, W. James and

many others, pointed out that the pluriformity of philosophies must lead to a legitimate pluriformity in thinking about the faith.[40] In the midst of all these upheavals some have pointed to the Orthodox Churches which are said never to have needed a reformation and can still manage with their old creeds. But there, too, the situation seems to be changing since the clergy trained after 1950 have a different view of their solidarity with Marxism than the older ones, not so well trained, and also because, particularly in university circles, there is a new questioning of the message of the gospel.[41] Just as this upheaval cuts across all the Churches, so it cuts across all countries. The problem is no doubt more pressing in English-speaking and Western European countries but it is also felt in such countries as Italy and Spain, Argentina and Mexico.[42] It is more alive among the young than among the old. Particularly the younger generation seems to be more aware of the margin of ideology which accompanies any confession, and of the manipulation of confessional formulas in teaching. They are no longer interested in confessing what their fathers confessed but in their own faith, just as their fathers long ago. They want to know what they really believe in.[43]

Within this context it is tempting to abandon the confession and its content altogether and to limit oneself to a practical Christianity, as it is called, as one can find it in the Quakers and the Salvation Army. Sociologists distinguish here between confession and confessionality.[44] Although the Quakers have no creed (perhaps because they have no baptism either), they quite definitely

---

E. Durkheim. Cf. the quotations from these authors in *Archives de Sociologie des Religions*, 27 (Jan./June 1969), pp. 37–50 and 73–7, together with the articles there by J. Seguy (pp. 28–35) and J. P. Deconchy (pp. 51–70).

[40] K. Rahner, "Schisma in der katholischen Kirche", in *Stimmen der Zeit*, 94, 7 (July 1969), pp. 27 f., and "Pluralism in Theology and the Unity of the Church's Profession of Faith", in *Concilium* (June 1969), pp. 49 f. (American edition, vol. 46, pp. 103 f.).

[41] Cf. the report in *Herderkorrespondenz*, 23 (Oct. 1969), "Atheistische Propaganda und orthodoxe Erneuerung in der Sowjetunion", pp. 462–5.

[42] For Mexico, cf. M. de Certeau, "Cuernavaca: Le Centre interculturel et Mgr Illich", in *Études* (Oct. 1969), pp. 436–40.

[43] See H. Keller, *loc. cit.*, p. 164. Cf. also the findings of the survey made by P. Villain and reported in "Les jeunes Français et la foi", in *Inf. cath. intern.*, 334 (15 Apr. 1969), pp. 4–6.

[44] Cf. N. Hasselman, "Ökumene und Bekenntnis", in *Bekenntnis in Bewegung, op. cit.*, pp. 113–16. This distinction was also noticeable in the

have a confessionality: a set of customs and practices such as abstention from alcoholic drinks, etc., by which they recognize each other's identity. Nor should we overlook the fact that those forms of Christianity which have no confession, all the same live, subconsciously perhaps, in a reaction to other Churches because these others have such a confession.[45]

4. *What are the Results?*

This question cannot be answered by pointing to the rare attempts made at drafting a really new creed. We must also take account of the growing consent about the necessity of such a new brief formula. Neither Pope Paul's creed nor Varillon's effort[46] is really satisfactory, though one should not overlook the fact that both demonstrate the recognition of the need for such a formula.

A second factor which is important for an honest answer to the question is that there is a greater and more informed awareness of the prerequisites of a new formula. These two factors, together with the attempts already made, should convince us that we are not in a blind alley, even though it may take long before we have more viable and better formulations of the creed, and these new formulas will also be provisional because they will stand in need of renewal in their turn.

(*a*) THE GROWING CONSENT ABOUT THE NEED FOR A NEW BRIEF FORMULA

This consent is more widespread in Lutheran Churches than in other ones. Lutherans have always attached more importance to their confession than, for instance, the other Churches of the Reformation. These others recognized each other's confession officially already in the sixteenth century. This implies that there

---

Assembly of the WCC where instead of talking about various "confessions" people referred to the "confessional families"; cf. *Ausschuss-Dokument*, 1, Glaube und Kirchenverfassung, p. 9.

[45] For the situation between Methodists and Anglicans, see J. Coventry, "Anglican-Methodist Unity", in *One in Christ*, 4 (1969), pp. 479–86.

[46] F. Varillon, "Un abrégé de la foi catholique", in *Études* (Oct. 1967), offprints available (26 pp.).

was already an understanding of the relative aspect of the confessional formulas.

The question arose again during the Nazi period in Germany when Christians were forced to realize that they needed a new confession to oppose this new paganism. Under the influence of Karl Barth theologians of the Lutheran, the other reformed and united Churches signed the so-called *Bärmer Erklärung* in 1934. The keynote of this Declaration was the confession of Jesus Christ and the renunciation of "German Christian" and pagan tenets. Something similar happened in the Dutch Reformed Church at that time.[47] After the Second World War the confession of the *Bekennende Kirche* was accepted by the Reformed Churches in Germany. The Lutheran Church, however, continued to oppose it. In the mission field a genuine new confession came into being of which the most independent version was that of the Lutheran Batak Church of 1952.[48]

The question is of little importance for the Churches with a pietistic character because the creativity of a "prayed" confession is very much alive there and the universal validity of the doctrinal implications means little to them. This holds, up to a point, for Anglican "comprehensiveness", although this did not seem comprehensive enough last year to allow the Methodists to join them.[49] The juridical facets of the confession in the sense of the taking of an oath were abolished last year in the Anglican Churches.

In the Catholic Church the need is felt most acutely by the groups that have sprung up spontaneously and among those for whom the liturgy is a happening. For the latter the proclamation by itself offers no solution, compels no adhesion, formulates no ideology and provides no strategy. It has no power in itself but releases power in the listener. For them the authority of the proclamation is not something given beforehand but must constantly

[47] E. Wolf, "Bekennende Kirche", in *Rel. in Gesch. u. Gegenw.*, I (3rd edn., Tübingen, 1957), cc. 984–8; for the Dutch Reformed Church see "Fundamenten en Perspectieven van Belijden", in *Documenten Ned. Hervormde Kerk (1945–1955)* (The Hague, no date), pp. 78–111, and in *Lebendiges Bekenntnis* (with an introduction by O. Weber) (2nd edn., Neukirchen-Moers, 1959).

[48] J. Hermelink, "Bekenntnis", VIII, "In den jungen Kirchen", in *Rel. in Gesch. u. Gegenw.*, I (3rd edn.), c. 1008.

[49] Cf. note 45.

prove itself in the actual and concrete relationships between man and man. People must in actual fact come to the faith and practise righteousness—a faith event.[50]

The need is also felt in many local Churches which attach more importance to their creativity and inspiration than to a centralized unity. Since Vatican II proclaimed the principle of the bishops' collegiality with the Pope as the holder of the Petrine office, the interest in the importance of the local Churches has increased considerably, and hence also the conviction that a reformulation of the "centre of the faith" is a necessity for these local Churches.

The question of what must be preserved at all costs obviously became an urgent issue for contemporary thinkers, such as Paul Ricoeur.[51] In this sense the Pope's creed can also be understood as a confirmation of the need for such a new formula. Moreover, the Pope himself shows this when he says in his introduction that his creed is mainly "a repetition of the formulation which is part and parcel of the immortal tradition of the holy Church of God", but "to which some explanations have been added because required by the demands of our age".[52]

(*b*) THE REQUIREMENTS FOR A NEW CREED

On the occasion of a new formulation of the creed by the United Church of Canada[53] Gregory Baum gave an outline of the requirements for such a new formula.[54] It must clarify the faith in a way which is basic and meaningful for the faithful and not only intelligible for theologians. It must protect the faithful against any form of superstition or unbelief which arises from the culture in which the faithful live. It must be able to fulfil a

[50] Such texts can be found in H. Oosterhuis, *In het voorbijgaan* (Utrecht, 1968); cf. Baumgartner, *op. cit.*

[51] *De l'interprétation* (Paris, 1965), pp. 37, 504, 509.

[52] *Osserv. Rom.* of 1–2 July 1968, p. 1.

[53] To give an example, this new formulation runs as follows: 1. Man is not alone, he lives in God's world; 2. we believe in God: who has created and is creating, who has come in the true man, Jesus, to reconcile and renew, who works within us and among us by his Spirit; 3. we trust him; 4. he calls us to his Church: to celebrate his presence, to love and serve others, to seek justice and resist evil; 5. we proclaim his kingdom; 6. in life, in death, in life beyond death, he is with us; 7. we are not alone; we believe in God.

[54] G. Baum, "A New Creed", in *The Ecumenist*, 6, 5 (1968), pp. 164–7.

liturgical function and therefore be able to be used as a prayer and be brief.

With Rahner[55] Baum underlines that a modern creed cannot begin abruptly but has to go back further than a creed used in a cultural period where such things as *revelation* and *God* are taken for granted as real, and this also holds for the way it is introduced in the liturgical celebration. It must also show how such a message liberates and saves, which does not necessarily do away with its aspect of being a "scandal" to the worldly mind.

Other authors add to this that a new formula must have a unifying influence on the Church and not lead to a schism. It must also have a doxological and a missionary character while it must remain suitable for catechetical purposes.[56] It is significant that the New Dutch Catechism, and also many other catechisms in Europe and America,[57] describe themselves as catechisms for adults. This presupposes that the creed must suit the needs of the age, have no pretensions to be absolute, and must be temporary. It will have to take note of the fact that a confessional language presupposes its own specific linguistic use. It is not meant to be the language of information but rather that of evoking a translation into living practice. This will make it more easily assimilable and prevent deviation into heresy in those who can only partially identify with such a confessional model.[58]

This leads us to a difficulty often pointed out by J. B. Metz, namely, that the difficulty of drafting a modern creed is too often and too one-sidedly seen as created by the formulation of *what* is being confessed. There is, however, a greater difficulty: the act of confession, which always implies a "remembering", becomes more difficult for modern man because he lives in a society which is "without history" and "without memory". But a creed is a

[55] "In search of a short formula for the Christian Faith", in *Concilium* (March 1967), although Rahner does not mention the problem of a new formulation itself.

[56] "Bewaltigen wir die gegenwärtige Glaubenskrise?", in *Herderkorrespondenz*, 23, 2 (Feb. 1969), pp. 49–53; *ibid.*, 23, 1 (Jan. 1969), "Bemühungen um ein Kurzformel", pp. 32–8.

[57] This will be extensively reported in the pastoral issue (3) of 1970 by B. Collins, F. Blachniki, O. O'Forman, W. Bless and L. della Torre.

[58] K. Rahner, "Schisma in der katholischen Kirche", in *Stimmen der Zeit*, 94, 7 (July 1969), pp. 20–33.

"remembering" and must be genuinely historical. This means that, if it is to have any effect on society, it must not remind us merely of the good things achieved by a past golden age. On the contrary, it must be a "dangerous" memory which reminds us of a past which left many things undone, often provided wrong solutions and brushed many others under the carpet.

If a historical religion such as Christianity were to transmit the past only as successful, in terms of an institution, it might give the impression that we have already achieved all that Jesus of Nazareth stood for. The provisional character of Christendom should remind us constantly that the past left us with many bills still to be paid for, and that the gospel commands many things which prevent us from taking either the State or the Church for granted, and so contain a threat to the institution. These things must constantly be formulated afresh because these mandates of the gospel must be more than a symbolic paraphrase of what we are conscious of today: they imply an effective criticism of society and this function can only be fulfilled in the Christian faith.[59]

Dombois mentions still another requirement for a new creed: it must have a legal character. Church law must always be guided by the confession.[60] The subject of this confession, however, is not an individual or a particular community, but only the ecumenical council as representing the real universality of the Church. The legal aspect of the Church stands or falls with the validity of its creed.

A last requirement was indicated by Vatican II where it speaks of a "hierarchy of truths".[61] The creed should make it clear that it attaches most importance to what is closest to the real kerygma, the nucleus of the gospel. A reformulation of this nucleus of the faith can no longer rest satisfied with the addition of further truths to the Apostles' creed. It must be more consciously reduced to the essence of the Apostles' creed, and concentrate on the true essence of the gospel.

[59] "Sinn von Bekenntnisformeln", in *Frankf. Allg. Zeitung*, 214 (16 Sept. 1969), p. 21.

[60] H. Dombois, *op. cit.*, pp. 695–9.

[61] U. Valeske, *Hierarchia Veritatum* (Munich, 1968); F. Haarsma, *De leer van de Kerk en het geloof van haar leden* (Utrecht, 1968); a commentary and bibliography on this expression can be found in *Suppl. Lex. Theol. K.*, II (Freiburg im Breisgau, 1967), pp. 29, 38, 88 f.

(*c*) THE RESULTS

This last point leads us to see an optimistic result in what at first sight does not look like a new formulation of the Apostles' creed but only a commentary on it. Ratzinger's book, *Einführung in das Christentum*,[62] takes the Apostles' creed back to the heart of the gospel in terms of our modern attitude to life. He does this in a manner which reveals a possible new way of being human. The style of the book never makes one forget that this Apostles' creed was of old the most used prayer formula apart from the Our Father. Reviews of the book[63] pointed out that it was not really a theology but rather a meditation. The question is whether this may not be precisely the best way of finding a new formula for the confession of the Apostles' creed in our time. This might well take us a step further in our developing consciousness and bring us closer to a creative new formulation. Ratzinger has been mildly criticized for having by-passed the principle of verification by reducing the question of truth to a question of love and thus having turned theology into a confession of personal commitment.[64] But it seems that Ratzinger's main aim was precisely to maintain the priority of faith over theology and to sound the various ways of reaching this faith. In any case, it remains a modern attempt at showing respect for the Apostles' creed. We would misunderstand the confessional character of the creed if we looked there only for the essence of Christianity.

Rahner has tried three times to achieve such a new brief formula of the creed.[65] The great merit of these attempts lies in that he at least has ventured into the dark night which besets our search for a genuine confession in our time. If we distinguish the brief formulas according to the level of people they are destined for, one may say that Rahner's attempts are suitable for those that have been philosophically and theologically trained. This is

[62] J. Ratzinger, *Einführung in das Christentum*. Vorlesungen über das Apostolische Glaubensbekenntnis (Munich, 1968). English trans., *Introduction to Christianity* (London and New York, 1969).

[63] H. Mynarek, "Das Wesen des Christlichen", in *Theol. Revue*, 65, 3 (1969), pp. 177–82.

[64] W. Kasper, *loc. cit.*, pp. 182–8.

[65] *Geist und Leben*, 38 (1965), pp. 374–9; *Concilium, loc. cit.*; *Schriften zur Theologie*, VIII, pp. 159–64; *Handbuch der Pastoraltheologie*, III, pp. 518 f.

pioneer's work which creates possibilities for a formula that can also function liturgically.

Apart from the already known formulations of a new creed[66] Baumgartner has produced an essay and a documentation on creeds that have a liturgical function.[67] The harvest is substantially richer in the Lutheran Churches. The episcopal conference of the VELKD dealt with this question from 30 September till 4 October 1969.[68] Its findings may be summed up as follows. In the course of history there have always been different ways of confessing Jesus Christ. This confession must be constantly renewed and expressed in new terms. The unity which links this pluriformity of confessions together is the confession of God's deeds of salvation. The historical creeds should not be neglected although the mere recitation and repetition of old creeds is not enough and induces a false sense of assurance. New formulations certainly constitute a risk but this has to be faced.

Schröer[69] and some others are mainly concerned with the practical aspect and emphasize the need for a new credal formula. If all ethics aim at a "communication of consciences" a new formulation of the Apostles' creed must develop the possibility of communicating through this creed. The creed here has its own opportunities, situated as it is between dogma and kerygma, christology and anthropology, ontology and personality. Here the accent clearly shifts in the direction of ethics just as in Catholic studies the accent has shifted from orthodoxy to orthopraxis.[70] In a survey of new credal formulas Keller[71] observes that not a single one

[66] See *L'espérance qui est en nous* (Rome, 1967), 38 pp.; F. Boerwinkel, *Voorlopig Credo* (Odijk, no date); E. Cardinal, *Protest achter prikkeldraad* (Amsterdam, 1968); *Hamburgse versie van het Apostolicum*, etc.

[67] J. Baumgartner, "Neubesinnung auf das Credo in der Messe", in *Liturgisches Jahrbuch*, 19, 2 (1969), pp. 91–112.

[68] W. Tannert, "Bekenntnis und Kirchengemeinschaft", in *Lutherishe Monatshefte*, 8, 8 (1969), pp. 393–7; cf. *Herderkorrespondenz*, 23, 9 (1969), pp. 402–3; *Bekenntnis in Bewegung*. Ein Informations- und Diskussionsbuch (Göttingen, 1969).

[69] H. Schröer, "Auf der Suche nach einer neuen dogmatischen Bekenntniskonzeption", in *Bekenntnis in Bewegung*, pp. 79–111.

[70] E. Schillebeeckx, "Het 'rechte geloof'—zijn onzekerheden en zijn criteria", in *Tijdschr. v. Theol.*, 2 (1969), pp. 125–48.

[71] H. Keller, *Bekenntnisbildung in der Gegenwart*, pp. 174 f.

bridges the gap between the world of faith and that of technology and the sciences.

The results may look meagre but it is in any case a gain that new ways are paved for the confession of faith which the coming generations will have to pursue to achieve a task which we, Christians, have hardly begun to tackle. As Theunis[72] says, to know this and to start digging is already proof that the faith is present and that there is hope.

[72] *Sprache und Wahrheit* (=Weltgespräch 7, Basle, 1969), p. 31.

Translated by Theo Westow

Biographical Notes

ARTHUR M. ALLCHIN, M.A., was born on 20 April 1930 in London, and is an Anglican priest. He studied at Christ Church, Oxford, and at Cuddesdon College. He is librarian at Pusey House, Oxford. His publications include *The Silent Rebellion: Anglican Religious Communities 1845–1900* (1958), and he collaborated in *Newman, A Portrait Restored* (1965). He is a contributor to *Irenikon* and *Journal of Ecumenical Studies*.

MYLES M. BOURKE was born on 30 January 1917 in New York, and ordained in 1942. He studied at the Catholic University of America and at the Pontifical Biblical Institute in Rome. With a degree in scripture and a doctorate in theology, he is professor of New Testament Studies at St Joseph's Seminary, Yonkers, New York, and associate professor of scripture at Fordham University. His publications include "The Meaning of the name Yahweh", *The Bridge*, Vol. III (New York, 1958), and he has written various articles on the New Testament.

ANTONIUS BREKELMANS, M.S.F., was born on 16 December 1930 in Holland, and ordained in 1958. He studied at the Gregorian, Rome, and obtained his doctorate in Church history. He teaches Church history at the theological college, Tilburg, Holland. His published works include *Martyrerkranz, Eine symbolgeschichtliche Untersuchung im frühchristlichen* (Rome, 1965).

MICHEL DE CERTEAU, S.J., was born on 17 May 1925 in France and was ordained in 1956. He studied at the University of Grenoble, the Catholic Faculty, Lyons, the Sorbonne, and at the Ecole des Hautes Etudes, Paris. He holds degrees in theology, philosophy and gained his doctorate in religious studies. He is a joint-editor of the review *Christus*, sub-editor of *Recherches de Science religieuse*, and a member of the editorial committee of *Etudes*. His published works include *Le Guide spirituel de J.-J. Surin* (1963), *La correspondance de J.-J. Surin* (1966) and collaboration in *Entretiens sur Henri Brémond* (Paris, 1967).

WOLFGANG DIETZFELBINGER was born on 12 March 1936 in Germany, and ordained in the Lutheran Evangelical Church in 1961. He studied at the universities of Munich, Heidelberg, Erlangen and in Rome. He obtained his doctorate in theology, and is the vicar at Erbendorf, Germany. His publications include *Die Grenzen der Kirche nach römisch-katholischer Lehre* (Göttingen, 1962), and he contributed to *Die Autorität der Freiheit* (2 vols., Munich, 1967).

BERNARD-DOMINIQUE DUPUY, O.P., was born on 21 August 1925 in Paris, and ordained in 1955. He studied at the Polytechnic in Paris, and at the Saulchoir. He is a reader in theology, and manager of the review *Istina* (Paris). He is the author of various articles on the episcopate, the *magisterium*, the laity, and Newman.

ENGELBERT GUTWENGER, S.J., was born on 6 June 1905 in Germany and ordained in 1936. He studied at Pullach, Germany, and Innsbruck, Austria. He doctored in theology and philosophy. He is professor of fundamental theology at Innsbruck University, where he was rector from 1961–62. His publications include *Bewusstsein und Wissen Christi* (1960), and *Wertphilosophie* (1952). He is a contributor to *Zeitschrift für katholische Theologie.*

JEAN-PIERRE JOSSUA, O.P., was born on 24 September 1930 in France, and ordained in 1962. He studied in France at the Faculty of Medicine in Paris, at the Saulchoir, and at the University of Strasbourg. He is a doctor of theology, and professor of dogma, and rector at the Saulchoir. His published works include *Le salut. Incarnation ou mystère pascal?* (Paris, 1968), and *Christianisme de masse ou d'élite* (Paris, 1967).

CARLOS-JOSPHAT PINTO DE OLIVEIRA, O.P., was born on 4 November 1922 in Brazil, and ordained in 1945. He studied in Brazil at the Major Seminary of Petrópolis, at the Dominican house of studies, Toulouse province, France, and at the Saulchoir. His publications include *Information et propagande. Responsabilités chrétiennes* (Paris, 1968), and *Evangile et Révolution sociale* (in Portuguese) (1963).

MORRIS WEST was born on 26 April 1916 in Melbourne, and is a Christian. After teaching modern languages in New South Wales, he became secretary to the Prime Minister of Australia. He is the author of such well-known books as *The Devil's Advocate* (1960), *The Shoes of the Fisherman* 1963) and *The Ambassador* (1965).

International Publishers of CONCILIUM

ENGLISH EDITION
Herder and Herder Inc.
New York, U.S.A.

Burns & Oates Ltd.
London, S.W.1

DUTCH EDITION
Uitgeverij Paul Brand, N.V.
Hilversum, Netherlands

FRENCH EDITION
Maison Mame
Tours/Paris, France

JAPANESE EDITION (PARTIAL)
Nansôsha
Tokyo, Japan

GERMAN EDITION
Verlagsanstalt Benziger & Co., A.G.
Einsiedeln, Switzerland

Matthias Grunewald-Verlag
Mainz, W. Germany

SPANISH EDITION
Ediciones Sigueme
Salamanca, Spain

PORTUGUESE EDITION
Livraria Morais Editoria, Ltda.
Lisbon, Portugal

ITALIAN EDITION
Editrice Queriniana
Brescia, Italy

POLISH EDITION (PARTIAL)
Pallottinum
Poznan-Warsaw, Poland